Published in 2021 by E-Book-It Publishing

This is a book of creative non-fiction. Historical figures and events depicted in this book are real. Any resemblance to characters portrayed, living or deceased, will hopefully provide an accurate and flattering rendition.

First Edition: 2021

E-Book: 978-0-9702563-3-1
Paperback: 978-0-9702563-4-8
Hardcover: 978-1-4566380-5-4

1.Creative Nonfiction 2) Family 3) Historical 4) The Greatest Generation

First Edition
Madisonville, Louisiana

Library of Congress Registration Number: TXu 2-245-118

Published by eBookIt.com

Other Books by Marie Louise Guste Nix

Visions of Splendor: Poems and Images of the Beyond in our Midst. ISBN 0—9702563—0 -2

Transportation to the Higher Place: Poems of the Way. ISBN 0—9702563—1—0

Restoring Soul: Poems of Healing Encounter, Awareness and Empowerment. ISBN 0—9702563—2—9

Being There: Reflections from the Scenes of the Mysteries of the Rosary. ISBN 978—1—4908—1984—6

Words of Praise for the work of Marie Louise Guste Nix

"Marie Louise's writing has very special qualities, which are quite unique and quite appealing. This book should have universal appeal."

Quote from a letter from **internationally acclaimed novelist Walker Percy**, who reviewed the novel prior to his death.

"Your books are a real gift! Your work is much needed today. So many are searching for truth and meaning beyond what the world offers. This is especially true of the young."

Reverend William Maestri, Former Superintendent of Catholic Schools, New Orleans, LA

"Highly readable. Many will relate to it and cherish it. Inspirational, the kind of work which will endure."

Chuck Vagnier, owner of Cover to Cover Books

"Marie Louise is very gifted. She has done a beautiful job. Quite an accomplishment!"

Ann Percy Moores, **daughter of Walker Percy** and owner of the legendary Kumquat Bookstore in Covington, LA, home of the Percy Family.

ACKNOWLEDGEMENTS

First, I thank all of the exceptional Professors of English at the Academy of the Sacred Heart and at Manhattanville College who instilled in me a lifelong respect for the power of the written word to make a difference in a life and in the world.

I will be eternally grateful to Walker Percy and the Percy family. During his lifetime, Mr. Percy read a rough draft and commented that the work should have universal appeal when complete. The Percy family supported me generously in launching my first publication Visions of Splendor: Poems and Images *of the Beyond in our Midst.* The success of that first launch gave me the foundation on which to complete and publish a trilogy and an additional book of meditations.

I'm deeply grateful to my readers near and far, especially those who have communicated gratifying affirmations. Close friends have sustained me in every way and friends of each book made it possible to keep going. My appreciation is boundless. Your loving generosity has been astounding.

Many thanks to all of the independent and major chain bookdealers who promoted my works and made it fun.

My dedication makes clear but I'll say it again: thank you Mother and Dad for the unforgettable, nutty adventures and lessons of life immortalized in *All This Closeness*.

ALL THIS CLOSENESS

By

Marie Louise Guste Nix

Impact Publications

DEDICATION

To Mother and Dad
With love and gratitude

and

To Young People Everywhere

Contents

FOREWORD

The Backdrop for the Story

This is a story about a wild and wacky family vacation, in which the Guste family takes an unexpected extended holiday, traveling by car 2,000 miles out of their way throughout the South of the Border country of Mexico. While it's a humorous and unforgettable episode, within the story is a message about the work we, as Americans, can do to become more aware of our neighbors in other countries and learn from them. It's a page in the larger story of a Louisiana statesman, William J. Guste, Jr. and his beautiful bride Dorothy Schutten, members of the greatest generation.

Dad was a pioneer champion of civil rights and social justice. The action in this narrative took place three short years after the Civil Rights Act of 1964 that outlawed discrimination based on race, color, religion, sex, or national origin. Prior to that we lived in a segregated society which greatly inhibited social mobility among African Americans and other ethnic minorities. Many young people today have little knowledge of such discrimination existing in recent history.

The 1964 law provided theoretical assurance of equality, but there would be decades of work to be done by thousands around America to implement changes in systems across every field and arena. Dad was one of the men and women who took that ball and ran with it till his death in 2013. Dad worked on legislation providing public housing for all, supporting Affirmative Action efforts in education, assuring the quality of health care for all by writing a new charter for New Orleans' Charity Hospital. The year following the events in this story, Dad would enter political life as a State Senator from New Orleans. Four years later he became the Attorney General for the State of Louisiana and revolutionized that office with unprecedented success as "the people's attorney."

In *All This Closeness,* William "Billy" Guste is seen with his large family moving along the road in a neighboring country with much to teach and learn about the American experience. The wisdom he shares with his children about creating a better world are useful and necessary today. We live in a world of instant solutions. But the gifts Dad shared with us come as more of a challenge: Open your heart, roll up your sleeves, extend your hand, work together and never give up.

During the years following his service in World War II, he plunged headlong into serving his community in New Orleans, Louisiana. Among other initiatives, he served as Chairman of the first Human Relations Committee in the City, and as Chairman of the Board of Lay

Regents of Xavier University which was then and is now the only black Catholic University in America. Dad's service as President of the Louisiana Housing Council formed a springboard for his work to fund the umbrella charity Unity for the Homeless. Dad helped establish the Monsignor Wynhoven Apartments, the first residence for low-income elderly in New Orleans. He served as President of the Associated Catholic Charities, President of the Cancer Society of Greater New Orleans, and President of the Metropolitan Crime Commission. He also served as the State Deputy of the Knights of Columbus.

In 1968, the year following the road trip chronicled in this narrative, Dad was elected to the Louisiana State Senate, and served from 1968-1972. In that capacity he brought the Model Cities program to New Orleans, organized the Louisiana Housing Council, fought for Urban Renewal legislation, authored Louisiana's Turnkey Housing Law, and established a special commission to investigate organized crime, among other initiatives.

My Mother was a full partner in every sense of the word and deserves equal credit for all of Dad's accomplishments. To this day, at 97 years of age, she can retell the story of pivotal conversations. She knew personally most all of the individuals with whom Dad crafted strategies for social improvement, graciously entertaining them at her table. Mother was an excellent listener possessed of keen intuitive wisdom about people. Her social intelligence, impeccable style and sense of humor brought her warm friendship with people of every type.

At the time the events in *All This Closeness* took place, I had begun a process of muddling through the confusion surrounding social problems and apparent injustice. I often observed my father at close range trying to figure out how he maintained hope and an unfailing positive attitude when the social problems he tackled were so deeply dysfunctional, and the inequities in society so blatant.

I had occasions to ask my Dad to explain the HOPE which fueled his efforts to tackle seemingly impossible problems like race relations in New Orleans. How was it he never seemed discouraged, frustrated or angry in the midst of such a battle? Didn't it seem overwhelming and hopeless? Young people then were being recruited by revolutionary groups and a year or two later, unrest over injustice would break out as urban and campus protests nationwide.

50 years later we once again hear the same outcry against injustice, which turned into a mighty roar after the brutal death of George Floyd. Though many advancements have been made to foster social mobility among those born in marginal situations and many victories won, major problems still confront us. Problems of multi-generational dependence on government programs continue. The unrest we witness today decries the divide still seen among the haves and the have nots.

The positive attitudes my father drilled into us as children were approaches which produced results. Working together for decades along with thousands of others, his prescription of hope moved us into a world where members of every race, color creed and sex are visible at the top of every profession in America. I invite young and old alike to revisit these timeless lessons as you move with our curious group through miles of rural territory, meeting our neighbors in the country of Mexico. The approach to bringing about change which my father embraced is the only one which will ever make a real and lasting difference. That was to choose hope, think big, work hard at it each and every day, never stop making friends and never give up.

With all of the pioneering efforts Dad worked on, his primary vision for a better world was based on a society of strong families. As his first daughter and the third of his ten children, I will never forget going with Dad to help bail out family homes which had flooded in Hurricane Betsy in 1964. I can never forget annually loading the car with Thanksgiving baskets and making deliveries to families in need. Dad would never be content with just delivering the gifts. He would accept a Coke and strike up a new friendship. I was amazed at Dad's ability to relate warmly to people from every walk of life. That was the gist of his method in bringing about social change. He didn't just give a man or lady a basket of food. He opened his heart to give them the gift of a trustworthy friend. Some of those friends would show up at the door on Christmas day, too. Not infrequently, Dad would receive phone calls during family dinner time from friends who needed work. He never rushed the call. For me and my siblings he created learning opportunities at every corner. Choose hope, and be the change in the world that you want to see.

In 1972, Dad became the Attorney General of the State of Louisiana and served five consecutive terms. He hired the best and the brightest lawyers, added an Environmental Division and a Consumer Protection Division. Dad's work in the Tidelands dispute brought $140 million in oil revenues to the State. EDUCATION: To fund two education trusts for the State, Dad negotiated a settlement with the Federal Government resulting in the release of $654 million in oil and gas revenues. INFRASTRUCTURE: He led a fight to bring $2 billion in Federal funds to the State for highway development. ENVIRONMENT: In the interests of a better environment, Dad led a fight to prevent superfund waste from being disposed of in Louisiana, and worked against destruction of Louisiana's estuarine. LABOR: Dad's legal expertise successfully blocked $260 million annual increase in rates. CONSUMER PROTECTION: Dad drafted the first Consumer Protection Law. With outgoing enthusiasm and front wheel drive Dad eventually became the President of the National Association of Attorney's General. He was respected and even loved by countless men and women of the law – professionals with strongly held positions which differed from his own. He could reach out and make a friend of anyone.

But more important than anything else was Dad's abundant joy in marriage and family life. Our life was robust with a house full of ten children and their friends who were always welcome. As partners, he and my mother together made the work of family life seem 100% positive, even fun. But the family life Mom and Dad designed was built on plans, ancient principles of wisdom and strategies forged lovingly and implemented jointly.

In *All This Closeness* I share with you some of the survival principles and positive thinking styles of a true leader and teacher tucked into the story of one hilarious family road trip. The misadventures of this family journey south of the border provided continuous opportunities for Dad and Mom to not only teach principles but to practice them against the odds. Day to day life during this adventure in a different country gave me images that impacted my mind and heart permanently. These images formed a relationship with RISK, with FAITH, with ADVENTURE, with DIVERSITY. During this survival adventure, the aphorisms and adages Dad always used became somewhat less annoying to me as a growing teenager. They became useful tools of wisdom which have greatly helped me through my own personal journey in life.

There's a reason I couldn't go to my grave without putting this narrative into a book.

The reason is HOPE that a few of you who are drawn to read our story will find one or two pearls of wisdom in its pages. And HOPE that most of you will get a dose of laughter the best medicine. In the world of today, we need it more than ever.

CHAPTER ONE

My father backed out of the driveway, squinting in the sunlight, looking over his shoulder. The chalk-white station wagon, a 1962 Ford, was laden down with nine of us, a couple of backpacks, a loaded red igloo, a water jug. On top, six red plaid American Tourister suitcases were covered with mustard colored canvas and tied to a chrome luggage rack with rope.

It's crazy hot in the first week of June in New Orleans, so bad you can see humid air sizzling up from the pavement and steam moistens everything and everybody. You really can fry an egg on the sidewalk.

To my parents, the chaos of a family vacation was perfectly good fun. In fact, there was hardly anything more wonderful and educational to do. And it was, it certainly was. Even so at 16, it began to feel a little suffocating. Much as I loved my numerous brothers and sisters, two weeks in a station wagon had started to feel like too much. And not entirely sensible.

"Well, is everybody happy?" Dad called a line which was a ritual kickoff for family outings. He called out the question in musical tones of the Jesuit High cheerleader he once was. The plastered smile, always exactly the same, seemed calculated to irritate. Who in their right mind would be happy in this jam packed carful of kids and their stuff?

I called him “Daddy” until that year, the year before my Senior Year, when it came time to switch to “Dad”. Just under six feet tall and of medium build, he had fair skin and curly hair which looked frizzed up when it wasn’t kept short and combed back with Vaseline Hair Tonic. He had olive green lawyer’s eyes, wore tortoise-shell glasses, and remained in motion constantly except when asleep, at the wheel or at the dinner table. He didn’t seem terribly good-looking to me, just admirable. My mother sure was wild about him—that was obvious. People of all types seemed to smile bright and stand straight when they spoke to him. He was good to people. He concentrated on teaching me about character and ideals, history and heroes. I agreed with everything in the program except the enormous amount of repetition. One thing was certain—you couldn’t forget those lessons. By the time he was finished with you, they were all definitely clear in your mind.

“Do you really think this trip is a good idea, Mother?” Anne asked with a quiet, serious tone. “Jimmy is already taking up too much room. I’m squinched.” At six years old she had a way of keeping an eye on everyone. Mother started up a “Hail Mary” quickly. Her serenity prayer.

“Okay.” Popped Dad. “Who has the map?” He rolled up his sleeves.

"Dad, we're not even two blocks from the house and you want to figure out where we are on the map?" asked Melanie.

"Dad, we don't need the map yet!" Chimed protesters from the back who didn't want to jostle around to find it.

"Don't tell me what we need, kids. I want to know where the map is. That means now!"

Disgruntled gremlins in back groped around moving paraphernalia and people to find it. "Somebody's sitting on it. Everyone lean forward!" I said. My job included bossing them when Dad wanted something done.

"I just got settled! Umpf!" Melanie forced herself over. "Let's take a look. I saw that map under the tote bag a few minutes ago." She went on huffing like it was heroic, shoving things aside to get underneath my overstuffed tote. She yanked it out before Dad started fuming. "Whew! Here, Dad."

"That-a-girl, Mel! Open it up and take a look at where we are."

"We're around the corner from our house." Melanie said. "Aren't we going to Baton Rouge? We know the best way to get there, don't we?"

"Of course, Melanie, but I need to make sure first of that we have the map. The right map. I want to be sure we're on the right track!"

"I see, Dad."

Mother fluffed up her shoulder length blonde hair as if engaged in an elegant conversation with the mirror. She had olive complexion, large chestnut brown eyes, and high cheekbones. We noticed she turned heads on the street. She kept a tiny waist too.

"Speaking of Baton Rouge, Billy, do you think we'll make it in time for the banquet tonight? Maybe we could just skip it."

"We'll see" The auto reply to questions he didn't want to answer.

"Shove over!" Valerie insistently demanded of Melanie.

"Over? What do you mean? I'm practically stuck to the door. I might be pushing it open! Thank God the lock works." Retorted Mel.

"I see all that space between you and the window!" Said Val, from the middle seat. She pointed out an inch of vinyl cushion between Mel's leg and the edge of the seat.

"Sure, Val. I'll turn and make sure my entire thigh is pressed against the window."

"I gave you that window! The least you could do is shove over!" Val fumed.

"I'm doing the best I can. Who says the window was yours to give away?"

"You're older so you think you deserve to get it. I had it before you got to the car. So I gave it to you. Understand?" Val shot back.

"I called the window from inside, and everyone heard me. Hey guys, didn't you hear me call the window?" There was silence. Mel groaned.

Mother established eye contact with my Dad and raised her eyebrows. She spelled out I-G-N-O-R-E as if her kids didn't know how to spell. The two of them smiled at each other.

"Do you mind if we stop at a gas station? I have to go." I said cringing before the response. It was always the same.

"Bathroom? Did you say bathroom? Marie Louise, what on earth is the the matter with you? We haven't been in the car twenty minutes and you want to go to the bathroom! Didn't I tell you all to go before we left? I don't understand it!"

"Mother makes us drink milk before we leave the house so it won't go bad. And I did go before we took off, Dad, I promise."

"In that case – we'll see."

"Let's say the Rosary." Mom suggested, prodding open the glove compartment. "Here, Melanie. Please pass the rosaries around the car." It wasn't your typical rosaries, it was the big, fat black ones the nuns wore hanging from their waists to mix with their black floor length skirts.

"Mother! We're not even out of town yet!" I was sixteen and would be mortified if anyone I knew caught me riding around in a car full of children chanting the rosary. It seemed mighty fanatical.

Melanie used a reasonable escape strategy. “Mother, don’t you think it works best when we’re out on the road a while and everyone gets irritable?”

“I just don’t believe this!” Jimmy, the one boy in the group, piped up. “I’m stuck in a car full of girls. It’s not fair!” He was eight, had curly brown hair and wore tortoise-shell glasses.

“Come on children, let the sunshine in. Everybody take a turn and say what they want. Let’s hear something positive, too!” said Dad.

“All I know is I’m with Marie Louise! I have to go to the bathroom too.” said Liz. She was ten, tall, blonde and athletic.

“If we’re supposed to say what we want – I want to go home.” Said Jimmy.

“Aw, Jim, you can do better. You know I need a young man around! Said Dad.

“Girls. Yuck!”

“I’ve got claustrophobia.” Valerie took her turn. “Push over Mel, and roll down the window! The air-conditioner isn’t working.”

“Valerie! Don’t be ridiculous. I’m going to make men out of you, and I won’t hear of anyone admitting of phobias. Ridiculous! Next?” Dad ruled on it.

"You say family trips are good for us, Mother, because they give us time to be together and get to know each other. But did you ever think that after all this closeness we might not even like each other?" I asked.

"Marie. You always get home from family trips with happy memories. You forget the discomforts and remember the fun, and all you saw and learned. After all, you can't take it with you!" What did she mean by that slogan of hers? It drove me up a tree. It was her answer to any aggravation. How could a slogan solve anything? You can't take it with you? Take what where? It was absurd.

"All this closeness. I wonder about it, Mom." I answered.

"Didn't I hear Daddy say we could take a turn and say whatever we want? My turn. I don't see why I have to sit way back here. It's no fair. It's hot." Anne complained.

"We need regular places or there would be too much confusion every time we got in the car." Mother explained. "If you're hot, you can trade places with one of the girls in the middle seat in a little while. I'll remind them. Next?"

"If nobody minds my asking, what time will we be in Baton Rouge?" Althea piped up. A teeny brunette of twelve, she moved about calmly and quietly, unlike the rest of us. She was light on her feet practicing ballet and tap routines in the living room.

Like an oasis of peace in a sea of chaos, Althea was an enigma to the rest of us.

"We'll see." Came the auto-reply. "Next?"

"It's nice of you and Mom to take us on a trip. I'm looking forward to it. Soon as we get there, we'll probably start having fun." Melanie said. I studied her with suspicion.

"I'll be a monkey's uncle! Now you've had a chance to say what's on your mind and get it off your chest. Let's hear a round of our State song. Come on gang! Let me have it, loud and clear!" He started it up as if in a stadium. To get it over with quick, we made a rolling boom box out of the wagon.

You are my sunshine, my only sunshine!

You make me happy when skies are grey.

You'll never know dear how much I love you.

Please don't take my sunshine away!

Dad smiled a big wide one. Mom took out smelling salts from her purse. In the city she wouldn't tolerate treating our station wagon as a sound truck, but she put up with it on road trips.

"That was great, gang! You've really got potential! said Dad, choking with pride.

"Now, Billy, let's say the Rosary. Please." Mother said, looking over at him, her neck straightening up. That evidently worked for her better than meds. Her prayers put the kids to sleep.

"Oh no, the Rosary?" groaned Jimmy and Anne, looking for a pillow to claim. It worked like their cue to take a cat-nap.

"The Rosary?" repeated Althea and Elizabeth. "Althea, think I could lay on your lap?" asked Liz.

"Yes. The Rosary. "In the name of the Father, and of the Son, and of the Holy Spirit, Amen. I believe in God...."

To say the Rosary, you recite fifty Hail Mary's in sets of ten, while meditating on special events in Jesus' life. I felt roped into it, but it was mechanical now and I had recited it daily after dinner for as long as I could remember. It wasn't so bad. I had plenty to pray for. Like deliverance! Maybe next year they'd let me stay home and work like my brothers Billy and Randy were doing this summer. They had it good. My parents had a different training program for boys and turned them loose more. They reined in on girls as if they might be dangerous. When Mother brought out the Rosary, I wanted to pray hoping it would work and they'd stop trying so hard to protect me, just start trusting me. What could be dangerous about me – an Honor Roll student, cheerleader and Student Body Vice-Pres?

Truth is, I had things to pray for besides the easement of my parent's big training program. I prayed that my football hero, a guy at

Jesuit, would call and invite me out, maybe fall head over heels for me. That my parents would let me apply to colleges away from home – that would take a miracle! No one in my family had ever gone away to college – not too far anyway. They figured with Loyola University four blocks away, why look anywhere else? It was Catholic, and it was the place where they met, so it had everything anyone could need.

I had plenty reasons to want to go away—to branch out and experience the rest of the world, meet people who weren't like us at all. I wanted to think through issues, realizing there wasn't an easy answer for everything. Hard questions wouldn't let me alone – like the problem of human suffering. I couldn't process such thoughts in the context of this family circus. My parents' well-intentioned reactions to philosophical issues were totally stupefying. They didn't understand my questions, worries, my search. Or what was happening to me as I read existentialist literature.

Sure, I could curl up warmly inside all the closeness I experienced with my brothers, sisters and parents. But there was another world out there that beckoned me.

My mother started. "The First Mystery, The Annunciation." Obligation and boredom mixed with yearning and a hunch that there was actually something to it. There was a lot to pray for too. Texas would be hot, the air-conditioner would break, someone would be sick, maybe me.

From where I sat, it wasn't a bad idea to ask God's help.

I began chanting the prayers. In spite of my best intentions I heard Mother's voice distantly as my head tipped over to rest on the warm glass of the highly prized window my sisters had fought to claim. In a dream state, I watched the mad scramble of packing up and getting out of the house that we had all survived one short hour ago.

"Daddy'll be home any minute now! Daddy'll be home any minute now! Daddy'll be home any minute now..." The sound rang in my mind over and over as I watched a vivid replay of the scene of our leave taking.

The dream went like this. Mother stood at the kitchen counter as was typical before a trip, calmly peeling fruits and vegetables for a last-minute snack. It was a centrally located peninsula, a perfect vantage point from which she could effectively direct everything going on in our four-story home. She deftly worked the paring knife between her thumb and index-finger, while monitoring what was taking place upstairs. Using the intercom, the new tech device with speakers around the house, she issued orders to each of her children about what to include in their suitcases. Calm and businesslike, she made necessary phone calls between conversations with children. A white princess phone hooked on her shoulder gave her both hands to work with as she sliced fresh fruit.

It was Memere on the line getting upset because she didn't know we were going anywhere. My father's mother didn't live with us but she might as well have been next door to us, she was so much a part of all of our family goings-on. Memere was a hyper-energetic and very classy porcelain teacup, pure French. Her widowhood looked like a roller coaster of non-stop activity.

"We didn't know we were going anywhere either until a few days ago. Billy has a meeting in Texas and we decided to make a short vacation out of it." Memere was used to coming with us on trips, or at least being invited and deciding not to come. I picked up the telephone on the second floor to call my friend Margot and say goodbye and heard my grandmother accelerating into full swing, jabbering a blue streak in Mother's ear.

"A vacation? Out of what?" She shrieked as politely as possible, acting astonished and miffed. "You mean you all are leaving town and I don't know a thing about it? This is a fine how-de-doo!"

"Mama, it's just the Housing Convention. It's over in Corpus Christi this year. We thought we'd take the kids to Astroworld too. The car is going to be crowded. We didn't think this would be your type of trip. Honestly." Mom was thinking about the last time they had invited Memere on a summer car trip and pulled up in front of the fashionable Carol Apartments to pick her up. She had three or four bags packed to the gills with stylish boutique clothes and medicines.

After taking a look in the wagon and attempting to find a place for her things, she had changed her mind and decided to stay home.

"Ever since we decided to take the children, I've been running around like a chicken with my head cut off trying to pack up and fold down the house." Mother never did run around like any chicken with its head cut off, but used these terms because it was a way of life for Memere, a woman of many involvements and events and community clubs. I understood immediately what my Mother, the mastermind of psychology was up to. She used the chicken with its head cut off as a defense strategy and to get a little sympathy. "You know how that is, Mama, admit it. You know how much we love you. Billy and Randy are staying home. They're working this summer, you know. Maybe you can all can get together one night."

"All right, then. Have a good time and be careful on the road. But Bootsie, please! Let me know when you're planning to leave town?"

"We will, Mama. We love you. Take care, and we'll see you next week."

Upstairs, there was a lot of shuffling, hollering and running around in and out of doors, and furniture getting bumped with suitcases and other people's thighs getting bumped with other people's stuff. It was like backstage at the opera between acts when the set is changing, everyone on their own treadmill and pressured.

"Please children, keep it down up there. This noise is not necessary! Come down here and drink some of this milk. Oh. While we're talking about milk, will somebody get up a note for the milkman and pin it on the side door?" Mom announced into the speaker.

"Mother! All this stuff won't fit in one suitcase. Althea wants to bring too much junk." said Valerie in a little fit.

"Cut out that noise and come down. We're only going for a few days. All you need is a couple of pairs of shorts, your bathing suit and toothbrush. Take out whatever else you have in there. Your father isn't going to want too many suitcases to load on top of the car. You and Althea can fit in one suitcase. No extra paraphernalia. Hurry it up. You know how your father gets when you all aren't ready. He ought to be home any minute now."

A variety of last-minute dilemmas were getting sorted out up there, so little wars would pop up like mini-forest fires. They came and went and we kept on like a gang of squirrels working together against time preparing for winter. Once the big boss was home, there would be no more time and anything you left you'd have to go without.

"Daddy'll be home any minute now!" No one in particular said this but everyone said it some time or other and with a different tone of voice. You could say it in a nervous way, hurrying and rushing distractedly, just with the idea of goading on any slackers. You could say it furious at someone who seemed bull-headed or just plain dumb on the subject of priorities. You could say it to plead with a sympathizer. "Listen, Daddy'll be home any minute now, could you run down and put this bathing suit in the tote?" Maybe you could even yell it out as a general announcement.

Valerie was grumbling about all of us going in one car and talking about claustrophobia. "Seven kids and two adults in one car. It's ridiculous! I have no idea how we're going to fit!" She griped, practically shouting. Most of us paid no attention to her distress, but Melanie tried to talk sensibly to calm her.

"Don't complain, Val. You're lucky to be going anywhere – don't you realize that? A lot of kids don't get out and see the world with a family they love. Come on, put a move on!" Mel sounded like a combination of Mother and Dad to me.

"Yes Val—move it! As soon as Dad gets home he'll ask me why you aren't ready. I'm not looking forward to making excuses for you." I said.

I went on to help the others zip their bags and pitch them over the banister to land near the side door where Julius was putting things in the wagon. Julius, the young creole father of two had joined our family circus as the handyman a couple of years back.

The traffic jam on the front stairs cleared and I tried to sneak down with my bulky white plastic hair dryer plus a puffy bag of pink foam rollers. I hoped that if Mom bumped into me the dryer would be mistaken for a tote bag. Mother was coming from the dining room and ran right into me at the bottom of the steps. There was no deceiving her.

"Marie Louise, I already told you we're not bringing anything extra. You can do without that. You have a short haircut, don't you?" Fact was, I had a Twiggy cut which meant it was like a boy's, only geometric. She had bought me the Sunbeam dryer before the new style.

"But Mom..."

"Go put it up then come down and drink some of this milk. I'm not leaving that milk in there to go bad. You need your calcium."

"Milk? Aw, Mom...uh...what about my diet?" I stammered.

"Foolishness! Did someone put a note out for the milkman?" She called out as she trailed up the steps, leaving me behind feeling deflated.

"The Second Mystery, the Visitation." Mother's voice broke through faintly.

"Oh no, he's home! I just heard the car drive up! Oh no, he's home! Oh no, he's home!" The sound hammered away on my mind loudly and reverberated as if coming from all different corners of the house. It seemed to come from the basement bathing suit rack, the kitchen, the solarium, the playroom, from Mama's bathroom, from the attic and the junk storage eaves.

"Get that suitcase downstairs! He'll go crazy if he sees this! Move!" I said to Elizabeth.

"I am. I am." Said Liz.

"Listen, Tina, I have to hang up. It's urgent. Bye." Melanie said.

"Where did my sunglasses go? I just put them down. This is absurd. Say a prayer to St. Anthony everyone. Those sunglasses cost me ten dollars and I absolutely cannot afford to lose another pair. This is ridiculous!" Said Mom.

"Mrs. Guste, where did you say you wanted this tote bag?" Julius had been a member of the family for about ten years since my father rescued him from his job as a short-order cook at the Toddle House Breakfast Shop on Claiborne Avenue.

"Just put it out on the driveway, Julius." Mother replied.

"Mama, I can't find another dry sock. All the laundry must still be wet." Althea wailed.

"Don't give it a moment's thought, honey. We'll pick some up out on the road." Mother was in the habit of buying cartons of Buster Brown socks, two dozen to a box. She'd buy two or three of those bundles without blinking an eye, figuring it was much better than going bananas every day searching for socks.

"Is that you, Billy?" Mom called innocently from the kitchen. "What took you so long? Didn't you say you'd be home at 2 o'clock? It's four. Is everything alright?"

"Yes, Butsie. I said I'd be home at two. I better go up and ask those children why all the suitcases aren't out on the driveway. There isn't a thing out there but one overnight bag. It's 4 o'clock! It'll be dark before we get on the Airline Highway. We're going to hit the 5 o'clock traffic head on." He charged up the steps tackling them two at a time with the demeanor of a firefighter in the heat of disaster – body angled forward, elbows bent perpendicular, hands clutched in fists. "I tell you people I'm coming home at two and here it is 4 and you're not even ready! Next time I'll have to tell you to be ready three hours earlier than I expect to leave. I want you sitting there at attention. No excuses."

Mom had by now moved on to pouring mugs of milk from purple and gold Walker Roemer cartons. She dialed up the dairy to cancel deliveries with the phone still propped between her ear and her shoulder. "All right, honey, all right." A wry smile broke over her face, as she placated his evaporating presence. "Here, Anne, have one of these tomatoes. They're wonderful for you. Full of vitamin C."

Dad reached the upstairs hall as I was coming out of my room with a pair of pants in my hands. I turned around to go back in my bedroom. He approached me and used two firm hands to guide me by the shoulders. "Come with me Marie Louise. I can use some help with packing." I was nabbed. He gave me a kiss on the cheek.

"I've got to go downstairs and get my pants pressed, Dad." I stammered.

"Pants pressed?" He responded with feigned amazement. "You had all day to do that! If they aren't pressed by now, you can start a new style." He said.

"Mama's not going to like me wearing them like this." I held up the pants.

"Where are my T-shirts? Did those boys come in here and take my T-shirts again? Outrageous!" He said, rooting through his sock drawer on his knees. "I can't understand this. Where are my socks? Can't you people put my socks in here together like I ask you?"

"Daddy, I don't...."

"Hang this shirt up over there, and get me some shirts out of the closet. Put them in that gray suitcase. Quick. We have to put a move on."

"These? Alright." With no idea which shirts my father wanted, I began going though them, handing him two blues, two whites and a yellow. "Okay. In the suitcase. We're good on shirts. What's next, Dad?" I said, starting to be amused.

While I packed the shirts as carefully as possible, my father disappeared into the bathroom and closed the door. He called instructions to me from in there. "Go get my seersucker suit and my tan suit and the navy blazer and pack those. Tell your Mother I need her up here. Be sure to hang those pants on the crease like I showed you, honey."

"Definitely." I called back smiling, my job about finished. I sauntered out of the room and pressed the button on the hall intercom to call Mom. I heard the hiss and smack of water hitting tiles, then the shower door slammed shut – whack – and I went back to my packing. Then came Dad's powerful voice crowing out one of his favorite back scrubbing numbers. It was an advertisement for the lakefront amusement park.

At the beach, at the beach, at Pontchartrain Beach,

You'll have fun, you'll have fun, every day of the week.

You'll love those thrilling rides,

Laugh till you split your sides,

At Pontchartrain Beach!

"The Third Mystery, the Birth of our Lord." The sound of Mother's voice could be heard faintly through a barrage of familiar noises of the scene back at the house.

Daddy was down in the driveway giving orders one after the other to anyone and everyone, acting like a firefighter in the heat of disaster. He enlisted our assistance with manners indicating urgency, as if the eye of a category 5 hurricane were three miles away and headed right for tree-lined Richmond Place. If you couldn't figure out a way to avoid Dad at times like this, you needed to be extremely busy, conscientious and occupied, behaving as if you understood the problem and the state of emergency. I ducked into the vortex of his presence gingerly, hoping for the best, but knowing it safer to assume there was hardly a chance of my doing the right thing.

"I'll take that young lady." He said. He approached me ominously, hardly aware of who I was, grabbing the bag and shoving it onto the small mountain of gear piling up on top of the wagon. "Let's shake a leg and get going, campers. Do you people realize it's already 4:30?" He called in a projecting voice. I practiced preventive defense by making an effort to appear panic-stricken myself.

"Oh my God! That traffic on the Airline! I'll run up the stairs and get those kids to come down. Don't worry, Dad. They'll be in that car in no time if I have a thing to say about it. Just watch." I countered, hoping to calm him some.

"Julius! Where is the canvas?" He loped over to the basement door and met Julius emerging cool, calm and collected with the brown cloth and the ropes.

"Right here, sir." He said with a smile. Julius seemed to enjoy the short duration of these chaotic moments knowing a few minutes later he'd be free to run the house on his own for a week.

Mother took her time with last-minute primping in her bedroom. No matter where she went, it was important to look her best. It wasn't other people she wished to impress. Contentment for Mom came with satisfying herself and her husband, and with being calm about things. Mother and Dad practiced avoiding each other on purpose at departure times. It was partly philosophical. Mother taught that a lady should never rush or appear to be in a hurry, because it might seem like your circumstances getting the better of you.

I returned to the driveway with all six of the others, and herded them into the wagon. Dad called out the window to my mother the words of a rehearsed script they used for trips. "Ready for take-off, Butz!" Her bedroom window was open so she could hear the cue. "Alright, gang, time for the serenade. You know the one I'm talking about! The birds in the wilderness."

Here we sit like birds in the wilderness

Birds in the wilderness

Birds in the wilderness.

Here we sit like birds in the wilderness

Waiting for Mother to arrive.

He played like a band captain starting up the half-time show at the football game. A minute ago, he was the overheated straw boss during harvest. The switch was crazy but made him seem lovable and funny.

Mother came down the stairs strutting with an air of one who had been waiting to be picked up, reading a magazine. She projected the persona of effective manager impeccably. Mom's rule—a lady doesn't get flustered, she handles it. Dad ran around in front to open her door.

"Is everybody happy?" That ridiculous question, somewhat like an adage, somewhat like an exhortation, somewhat like a veiled order, came drumming through my head repeating itself over like the nervous, automatic pecking of a woodpecker.

"Well, yes!" came the half-hearted response of the troop. We knew perfectly well the answer he was looking for, and knew not to bother trying anything else.

"Louder, gang, let me hear it!" Came the cheerleader again.

"The Fourth Mystery, the Presentation of the Child Jesus in the Temple." By this time, Mother's voice was but a weak strain, but it still had strength enough to calm the yelling going on in my mind.

Now I saw the re-play of the Ford wagon rolling down Richmond Place again, with all of us inside griping and complaining, squirming and conjecturing, getting adjusted to our new habitat. I heard the comments over again, watched the search for the map, saw myself begging to go to the bathroom and Mother's cheekbone tipped forward as she leaned forward to open the glove compartment for the rosaries.

"The Fifth Mystery, the Finding of the Child Jesus in the Temple."

Next thing I knew, Dad was pulling to a stop aside white columns of the Bellemont Hotel in Baton Rouge. I straightened up and shuddered, turning to find all the other disciples drowned in a deep and seemingly peaceful sleep.

CHAPTER TWO

In this environment of chaos and confusion, I began to come of age.

"Listen, gang! I'd like to show you children every inch of the greatest country on earth. Teach you something along the way, too." Dad called out poking his index finger straight up as though it were a country teacher's pointing stick. Reaching under the seat for my copy of *The Grapes of Wrath*, I made an effort to keep a straight face and hold off from choking out loud. I was learning quite a bit about our country, its benefits as well as its evils in pages which became my home for better or for worse. Engaged in fiction, I loosed my shackles and traveled the continents.

"It's being close together that makes a trip a joy to me." My mother answered. Thomas Hardy's *Far From the Madding Crowd*, next on my list, was tucked in the backpack, along with *The Fountainhead*, by Ayn Rand. There was so much to ponder and analyze. Opening my mind to alternative ideas and entering a personal search for meaning seemed like part of becoming fully human to me. That wasn't so obvious to those around me, and so I began to appreciate a rare patch of solitude. Easy answers drove me further into mysteries and a long journey lay ahead in various ways.

"Getting away for a week together is good for us. We have a chance to get to know each other." Mother continued. "There's nothing quite like it—you become a pioneer family. You learn to appreciate the comforts of home, too."

Pioneer family? I thought. Oh my God! There was a whole lot of dying on those trips out west, wasn't there? My pioneer days needed to end soon, one way or another. I was sixteen—that should tell you my days were numbered when I could go along politely. I couldn't wait till they would let me stay home and work as a lifeguard during the summer. I contemplated the Joad family in Steinbeck's novel long and hard and realized that no one chooses the family they are born into. But everyone survives it and emerges with some type of toolkit.

Mother ran her fingers through her strawberry blonde wavy locks. "What is it you're meeting with the Governor about, Billy?"

"Creating a Charter for Charity Hospital, Butsie. We've needed it for years. Remember? John appointed me Chief Legal Advisor for Charity Hospital."

"It's coming back to me. You were awarded that plaque at the banquet last year with the key to the city. Right?" Mother reached in her purse and pulled out the powder compact.

"Don't worry about it, sweetie. I'm meeting with the Governor tomorrow. Let's hope he approves the draft. It's taken me hours and hours of work. I'm pleased with it but ready to get it out of my hair."

"There's a charter in Dad's hair!" Jimmy called out.

"Your father never stops doing for others, children. I couldn't stop him if I tried."

Why did she have to speak to us all as "children" when I had long ago stopped thinking of myself as a child? Does a child go on television to advertise for a city-wide Leukemia Drive? Does a child get a job as a lifeguard at a summer camp? I think not.

"I'd give anything to get him away from all these problems once in a while." Mom said.

"You mean the problems of the world?" Melanie asked.

"Yes. The problems of the world." She sighed. "Sometimes you work too hard, Billy."

My father pulled up in front of the State Capitol and parked.

"Pile out people.[1]" He called loudly.

"Everyone stick your shirts in and pass this comb around." Mother said, bending over to work with Anne. Dad gave a forward march signal with a flick of his wrist in the air and a smile. I cringed at Dad's weird gesticulations. He strode up the multitude of stairs cascading out

---

[1] Siblings traveling: Marie Louise, 16, Melanie 14, Valerie 13, Althea 12, Elizabeth 10, James 8, Anne 6.

from the doors of the State Capitol Building. As soon as he was angled forward and moving up, Jimmy placed a lump of fake dog-doo in Anne's white patent leather purse.

"You can use this if we meet anyone important." He whispered to her. Five yards of children followed behind Mom and Dad in relative quiet. The heat made it almost impossible to speak even if you were standing still. Trudging up those stairs reminded me of the Myth of Sisyphus, the poor devil pushing and shoving his weighty stone up that God-forsaken mountain and never getting anywhere. Add to the workout the pranks my brother set up, the temptation to hiss, simultaneously mixed with the urge to break out in laughter. Surrounded with respectable characters coming and going I resigned myself to behaving as camp counselor for the youngsters I happened to be with. I thought perhaps there should be pay associated with this task.

We reached the top of those forty nine steps breathless and taken aback by the sight of two monumental bronze doors which faced us. The magnitude and detail in the artwork depicting the history of Louisiana from Bienville to Huey Long stopped us in our tracks as if we'd be sprayed with a stun gun.

"How come we've never seen these doors before, Dad?" Mel broke the silence.

"We're seeing them now." My father replied.

"I didn't know we had anything like this in Louisiana." Val added.

"Well we do. It should make you proud. And in a few moments, a tour guide will take you all around the entire building and tell you a little bit more about our government and the way it works." Dad responded, yanking open the right door.

"Hope it's just a little bit. Can we get cokes in there, please?" Jimmy asked.

"Sure. Just behave, alright? I won't be too long, maybe an hour. Butsie, you can stay here and wait for the tour guide and then after you've seen everything, go for cokes in the cafeteria downstairs. Meet me in the Governor's Office on the 4th Floor in an hour. He'll be happy to meet the children." He kissed her and disappeared.

Mother, the naturally gracious Southern lady, stepped up to the information desk and I led the monkeys over to the center of the stone and marble hall to view the ten foot wide State emblem sculpted in bronze on the brown marble floor. The same silence settled over the troop as had gripped them at the sight of the front doors. What a new view of Louisiana this was. Though we had been to the Cathedrals of New Orleans, the Cabildo, and the museums in town, to find something stately and majestic, artistic, lavish, and fine, seemed rare outside of New Orleans.

"Keep yourselves in order, please. Listen to the guide and learn." Mother instructed quietly upon rejoining the group.

Momentarily, a young tour guide appeared and began speaking to us of our colorful history, and the seven of us traipsed around behind her as though balancing china plates on our heads to earn supper. Thus my father's wagonload of ornery travelers drank in a bit of local culture and history. We toured the Senate and House Chambers, took seats in the balconies and heard issues being discussed. We peeked in the Conference rooms, passed the representatives offices and before long were returned to our starting point near the State Emblem. I wondered how long I would have to wait before I could have a job in the State Capitol.

Mother handed the young woman a dollar. "Get yourself a coke, sweetie. We appreciate the lesson. You had them listening, too!"

Jimmy and Anne took off running the length of the hall in a race. Mother's mouth dropped open and I took off on a rescue mission in a flash. Kids, I thought. You never knew what could be coming next. How did mother do it? It must be those maxims she uses, I thought. They didn't seem to make much sense to me but if they helped her stay calm, what could be so wrong with them?

Just before noon we boarded the elevator. In an era when excellent personal service was a goal of every business, these gentlemen, and mind you they were always men, stood tall and proud in impressive maroon uniforms, gold trim and tassels at the shoulders. Their posture, dignified welcome and courtesy showed they were well trained ambassadors of the community spirit of Louisiana in our State Capitol. These men also supervised orderly conduct and made sure that guests went where they were welcome.

A lanky young man nodded at my mother as we stepped aboard.

“Fourth Floor please, young man.” Mother put in with a nod in reply.

“Bu Ma’am.” He replied wincing. “No one is allowed to get out on the fourth floor. Only by the special invitation of the Governor himself can anyone get out on the fourth. It’s the Governor’s private offices.” The young man looked us over again slowly and turned to interact with his panel of buttons. Repulsion seemed apparent in the way he hoisted his right shoulder blade. As he swiveled his body around to face the buttons, I saw a look break over his face as if he smelled a bad egg. I understood that we didn’t look the part of anyone the Governor would be likely to summon and want to do business with.

A mistress of silent signals, my mother kept her dignity. She had a look for every situation. There was that look she’d use when she’d catch Dad rummaging through the trash out back. One look in the eye and he’d respond peaceably, straighten up and walk away smiling like a kid caught in the cookie jar. The look she saved for elevator boy was one of silent authority. She looked into his youthful eyes and he proceeded to do whatever she told him.

"Thank you, young man." She said, stepping out of the elevator. "Children. I expect you to be on your best behavior."

Governor John Mc Keithen was over six feet tall and built between the slender and medium category. He was fair skinned, with wavy reddish blonde hair. Stepping toward us he approached my mother, cavalierly kissing her right cheek according to Louisiana French custom. I stood tall, holding my stomach in, chin up and chest out. Maybe I could get a job working here next summer, and it might make this trip worth it. My mind raced to the point where I had to restrain myself from blurting out the question about job openings. The Governor turned to me next after my mother.

"What may I ask is your name, young lady?" He looked me in the eyes with a warm glow on his face. Wow! I saw how he made a success of his campaign with a slogan everyone considered sort of ridiculous and countrified. In the television spots he would face the voters, smile and ask "Won't you hep me?" When the tall handsome Governor leaned toward me to ask my name, his looks and manner were disarming and engaging. He made you feel comfortable and convinced of his genuine interest.

"I'm Marie Louise." I replied. "I'm happy to meet you, Governor Mc Keithen." He patiently proceeded to interview each of Butsie's children, spacing pithy remarks and courtesies in a stylized but relaxed manner, as if he could never tire of being interested. When he came to Liz, who stood next to my brother, Jimmy began picking his nose. I stuck my elbow in Melanie's rib cage and pointed at the daredevil. My face was hot and I wanted to kill him, but all of a sudden everyone in the room was holding their sides and shaking. The Governor then handed me an 8x10 glossy photograph of himself and I was nudged out of my state of shock.

"Do you mind signing your picture, Governor?" I asked. Great proof for my Civics teacher next year! A few extra points at least. He went to his breast pocket for his gold Cross pen and quickly scrawled his signature with a grand flourish.

"How about mine?" Said Mel.

"And mine.

"And mine" came the rest, in a clamor.

"The Governor has a luncheon meeting, I'm sure. John, thank you, but there's no need...."

"Don't worry your pretty head, sweetheart. I'm enjoying all these beautiful children of yours, Butsie."

Children. That couldn't have meant me. Children. Definitely not. He had addressed me a moment ago as "young lady".

"Let me see if I have anything else to give y'all." He turned to his desk to look around. "Oh yeah, I got some new matchboxes with my picture on the inside cover and the state bird on the outside. Which one of y'all can tell me the name of the Louisiana State Bird?"

"The pelican!" The gang called out in unison.

"Ah ha! Billy really taught 'em a thing or two. Now here are some doubloons from last year's Mardi Gras Ball in Washington, D.C. Oh yeah, and here—I've got some balloons for you too." He handed me a fistful of royal blue latex jumbos with a yellow and white pelican stamped on.

Back in the elevator, I sensed a buzz of energy. Being there for even a few moments opened up a new horizon to me, one filled with opportunity. How did Mom and Dad pull that off? And she acted as if it were no big deal.

"John Mc Keithen is much better looking in real life." She said with sparkling eyes. His television ads don't do him justice, Billy." In the summer of 1967 Mom and Dad were still private citizens and Dad had never taken a run for public office. That would change the following year after Dad received a phone call asking him to run for State Senate to replace Charlie Tessier. Two years later, Mom and Dad would know most everyone in Louisiana State Government.

"Never thought about it, Butz." My father replied.

"The sport coat was alright but the slacks needed some altering. They were too tight on him. Honestly, a man in his position needs someone looking out for all that."

"I suppose so." Dad responded.

Mother went on with the issue. "Did you notice, Marie Louise? Those slacks. They were tight and too short. You would think his wife could help with that. Shows you everyone's human!"

"Now that you mention about his pants you're right, but he was a dreamboat." I said. "Who would've thought it with that country T.V. ad?"

"Will you shut up, you creep? Said Jim.

"I'm surprised at you, Jimmy. If I've told you once, I've told you a thousand times, you children are absolutely not allowed to say shut up. And that's that." Mother said emphatically, eyeballing him.

"Sorry, Mom." said Jim, hanging his head, casting a venomous glance in my direction.

Headed on to Houston the clamoring about swimming broke out.

"Can we go swimming as soon as we get there?"

"Daddy, can we go swimming as soon as we get there?"

"Daddy, Daddy...."

Daddy was lost in thought, and a probing, penetrating look came over his face.

When he was in that state, you couldn't get answers to any of your questions, even a "we'll see." You couldn't even be sure he had heard you. I knew that, but my sisters and brother wouldn't give up, not for an urgent matter like swimming.

"Daddy, can we go swimming as soon as we get there?"

Again, my father played deaf. Jimmy tapped his shoulder. Getting no response, the poor guy turned beet red with frustration. He began shoving and gritting his teeth.

"Daddy!" he hollered. "Give us an answer!"

"Jimmy. Leave your father alone. He has a lot of things to think about. Children, relax. The water will be there when we arrive." Mother placated.

"Good. The answer's yes. O.K. I can deal with that."

"Keep down the questions and stop worrying, Jim." Mom went on.

"You said the pool will be there, Mom. So that means yes." Elizabeth said.

"Maybe." She replied.

"Oh come on."

"Butsie, where's the map?" Dad asked, emerging from the think tank. "I don't want to get lost on this expressway. I'm ready for a nap."

1967 was the year Twiggy hit the front cover of Time Magazine, Vogue and Mademoiselle. Suddenly we were all supposed to look emaciated. I spent the year fasting behind Mother's back, so that by the time summer rolled around I was skin and bones. Friends were starting to worry about me but I loved was the feeling that boys were staring at me. Now that I think about it, maybe it was the crazy colors I'd wear they were staring at – not my lack of curves! That was the year of paper dresses sold in pop-open tin cans, and mini-skirts. Mom didn't think much of throwaway dresses, so she didn't bother buying any for me. The ones I'd pick out at Lerner's may as well have been for one-time use, they were so cheaply constructed and flimsy. When I started to want more clothes besides school uniforms and church dresses, Mom enrolled me in a sewing course and offered to pay for fabrics, so long as I finished one number before getting fabric for the next. I cringe when I think of those skin tight orange and hot pink flowered pants I threw together from a Simplicity Jiffy pattern, and wore with a pink knit halter top. Pink plastic sunglasses put my look over the top and I felt really cool.

"You think you look good in those cheesy sunglasses?" Melanie asked me.

"What's the matter with my new shades? Jealous?" I responded.

"How much did you pay for those, about ninety-six cents?" I picked up my rumpled copy of *The Grapes of Wrath*.

"Ninety-nine cents to be exact. You can't tell me they're not a perfect match for my new pants." Althea and Elizabeth began giggling viciously. I ignored them all, flipping open my paperback book.

"Not to make you feel worse, kiddos, but I even got a pair of yellow ones the same day. They were selling like hotcakes. I wouldn't dare take a chance and let them sell out. They look exactly like the ones selling in Gus Mayer for four-ninety five."

"Leave it to Marie Louise. The philosopher queen!" Melanie answered.

"No kidding. They're hot. I hate to make you feel bad, but Cheryl Tiegs had some like this on when she modeled for the cover photo for Teen Magazine!" I explained, unperturbed.

"Am I supposed to be impressed? I could care less what that floose-ball wears!

And ask yourself – how many other groupies went out and bought the exact same pair for the exact same reason. You're making a fool of yourself. You're a conformist, and you don't even know there's something wrong with that." Mel shot back.

"Eat your heart out." Nothing could make me question my allure as long as I weighed ninety nine pounds. "Have you read any good books lately?"

Getting our stuff out of the wagon at the Holiday Inn, Dad hooked a couple of overnight bags on my shoulders. Turning into the suite at the Holiday Inn, I found the girls sprawled out on the beds. My father was following me.

"Can we go swimming now, Daddy? You've got to hear us now!"

"As soon as Marie Louise gets her suit on!" Dad nodded with a smile.

"I thought I'd take a nap, Dad." I replied.

"You can do it. Take your book out there." He disappeared into the adjoining room and closed the door.

My multicolored tank suit was as loud as a neon sign which was good for proudly showing my emaciated body. Mother forbid us to wear low-cut clothes and I was pretty flat chested anyway. I chose a swimsuit that was so skimpy in the rear that it barely covered my behind. If she noticed, she didn't comment.

My sisters and brother had dashed out to the water the instant they heard my father instruct me to get out there. I peacefully assembled my pool gear – baby oil for frying myself, towels, pink sunglasses and a cup of ice.

"Cow...bung...ah!" Came the howl just before a tidal wave covered me with cool chlorinated water from the pool. "Yeow...." A giant sploosh and the pent-up kid had his moment of relief.

"Splish splash I was takin' a bath..." Jim shimmied around imitating Chubby

Checker before another double flip off the diving board. I looked over at Allie who was draped in soaking travel clothes sticking to her small body.

"Think you could put on a swim suit, Althea?" I glared at her. "New style, huh, swimming in your clothes?"

"Like I had a choice. Tarzan over there threw me in when I came out to look."

"Here. Go ahead in and get your suit. I'll be here." I threw her my towel.

Lowered down on the chaise lounge with a skimpy white towel from the room, I covered my limbs with baby oil. Situations like this required called for the glamour of perfect posture. Behaving as though a yardstick was glued along my spinal cord did the trick. The idea was to act cool, relaxed, refreshed—no matter how scorching the heat. Two young men who had been horsing around on the opposite side of the pool eyed me applying oil and came to settle themselves on the chairs beside me. I ignored them, adjusting sunglasses and flipping open Steinbeck. By accident, I noticed one of them was good looking.

"Great sun today!" The cute one got up the nerve to talk to me while his sidekick looked over to see if I'd be friendly. Before replying, a heap of ice landed on my chest. From Jimmy. I behaved as though I was not surprised. I cast him a glare of reproach, then turned to the new friend on my right.

"Nothing quite like it – June!" I smiled at him.

That night under the covers I kept company with the Joad family of Steinbeck's epic novel *The Grapes of Wrath* as they traversed the Southwest in poverty. It was an eye-opener, a heart opener, laden with mysteries which remain unsolved for every thinking human. The passage from Scripture, "Blessed are the poor..." seemed enigmatic and plagued my conscience for years to come. That was before I understood the words as a way of life and a mandate. How it was possible to become poor if one was not? Were you supposed to try and become poor? Were there were other meanings to the Lord's exhortation, like a poverty of choices or of control? Like everyone else, I had nothing to say about the situation I was born to, who my parents were, how many siblings they gifted me with, what religion they raised me in. I had no say in the role which was assigned to me in this group, or what tools I had to work with to shape my own destiny. No choice had been given to me as to which gifts or defects would define me. Nor was I consulted as to what would be my height and chemistry, my skin color, my predispositions and natural aptitudes. In ways, Butsie and Billy's troop wasn't entirely different from the Joad's—in being human, bonded by God, Mother Nature, destiny, in defining one another, moving in God's mercy, in vulnerability to what was inevitable. But the radical differences were haunting, the Joads being a family of impoverished migrant workers, and the Guste clan emerging from middle America. The story of the Joads imprinted my heart and my life with deep concern and a mandate to discern what God expected me to do to help.

"Who is the prettiest in the family?" Anne started a game which she thought might make the night fun.

"Go to sleep everyone." I said, dog-earing my Steinbeck.

"Come on, it's fun. O.K. Everyone say what they think!" Anne went on.

"What else is there to do? Are we supposed to read books in June like Malouise?" said Val. "So I vote for Melanie."

I closed the book and fluffed the pillow. "This game may be offensive. Go to bed." I said.

"Mal is jealous. And you're crazy, Val. Everyone knows Mother is the prettiest." said Anne.

"Who is the ugliest?" Elizabeth called out. There came a barrage of suggestions, insults and counter insults."

"I told you all – go to sleep!" I was about to lose my cool.

"Who has the best sense of humor?" Melanie crowed.

"I know who has the worst", said Jim. "It's Elizabeth. She can't take a joke."

"Can too. How dare you say that to me, you brat?" Liz retorted.

"It's just that no one can tell you anything – ever. You think you're so great, but hey. You're not as terrific as you think!" Jimmy shot back.

"I'm getting there. Just because I'm the best at basketball, that shouldn't bother you, Jimmy."

"Who has the prettiest feet?"

"Who sings best?"

"Who is the best organizer?"

"Who is fattest?"

"...most unique....best sport....most brave....goody goody.... thinnest hair?"

Each of us had a sympathizer and a champion in this game and the net result was each one got some recognition and some exposure to insult.

I wondered to myself if this was what Mother was referring to when she said that a family trip helped us to get to know each other and sweat each other out. Did all this closeness work to keep a family together, or spin us far into the universe later on?

"Let's get up and at 'em, guys! Houston's out there waiting for us and there's lots to see and do. Time's a wasting!" Dad accidentally slammed the door leaving out of our room. I automatically got up to pass around the room stripping sheets off of each of my sisters and my little brother.

When Gene Wilder starred in the movie Frankenstein, he may have invented his mannerisms in imitation of my father. It was a method of being possessed and excited about whatever you were doing in the present moment, blinded by enthusiasm and zest so that all else faded into the background. It seemed unreasonable, unnecessary and downright foolhardy to me, but being highly kinetic helped him get things accomplished. It was true, when I thought about it, he did manage to behave in a serene manner on occasion while lost in a good mystery novel. Considering this, I deduced that the front wheel drive was a deliberately chosen means of mobilizing a troop. Calculated or not, his ways were a laughable riot to his children.

"Good morning, Val. Morning Liz. Morning Mel. Morning Jim. Hey there, Anne. And you over there, Mel. Don't you love mornings? Up and at 'em, sportsfans."

"You forgot me, Althea said climbing out. "And I'm the one you can count on."

She came over and gave me a kiss.

"Hey, it's cold in here. I need that sheet." Mel put the pillow over her head and dragged the blanket up under her chin. She expected to come off unscathed in any blitz attack by Dad when he came in acting like there was a fire.

"Get out of that bed immediately!" I told her.

"I'm getting out soon. Promise." Dad came in.

"Why aren't these kids dressed, Marie? Get out of that bed immediately, Valerie.

I'm going to the Pack-a-Sak to get some milk and donuts, and I want to leave out as soon as I get back." He tore out like Daddy Warbucks. As the door slammed behind him, I appeased his shadow.

"Okay, Dad. Okay. Just calm it down. We're going to make it, I promise." I shuffled about tapping people and looking at my watch. Driving and swimming made for a deep doze. I grabbed the chance to get into the bathroom along with Althea, calling from in there to Valerie. "Is Jimmy awake yet? Stay on top of it Mel, or we'll never get out of here. Get up, Jim."

"I think he's coming to. I just poked him and he grunted." Called Val.

"Donuts will be here any minute." I called from the bath. "C'mon everyone, get with it."

"Donuts?"

"Donuts?"

"Donuts!" Why hadn't I thought of that before? "Yes, Krispy Kreme donuts. If you're dressed you get one, too."

Val began putting in a bit of help. "If you don't get up this minute and get dressed, Elizabeth, I'm wearing your shorts." Liz rubbed her eyes and rolled off the bed.

Mother overheard this from her adjoining room where she was having her cup of French Market Coffee and Chicory. Coffee from anywhere else but in New Orleans seemed like nothing but muddy water, so she brought her own electric percolator and our famed aromatic ground coffee in the red and blue package from Café du Monde down by the Mississippi River.

"Good morning in there." She called. "Remember, the first one up is the best dressed." She chuckled and took another sip of her coffee. I never observed my mother shuffling around in the morning trying to make sense of her hair. From what I could tell, she woke up fully dressed.

Elizabeth sat up and glared at Valerie. "Don't even think about wearing my new shorts. I just got those. You have the nerve to threaten me?"

"My, my, Elizabeth. I do say, aren't you a little hostile this morning? It's only a pair of shorts! And I helped you get out of bed, didn't I? You owe me." Val said, enjoying the scene.

"What makes you think I wanted to get out of bed? I don't like having to get up just to defend my stuff, either." She scowled and began pulling on her clothes.

Mother overheard it. "Laugh about it, Liz. You know, you can't take it with you! Take it with a grain of salt. Like water off a duck's back. Don't let it get you!" At the very least, she lived by her principles.

Dad burst in on the scene with a couple of brown bags and was stampeded by his herd. The armful of brown bags were opened before they made it to the dresser top.

"Breakfast, everyone!" he looked around to find that some were still in bed.

"Do I believe my eyes? What have you all been doing? Marie Louise! What's going on?"

"I tried, Dad."

"Trying isn't good enough. You'll find that out in life."

"They're tired. Come off it, Dad. We're supposed to have fun, right?"

"We can have fun seeing Houston. I just want to get going."

"Dad, give me a break once in a while." I went over and took his hand. He tousled my boyish haircut and gave me a hug and kiss.

Melanie peeked out from under the blanket. Noticing the little parent-teen moment going on, she slithered into the bathroom.

"What on earth is Melanie doing? Couldn't you get her out of bed?" Dad asked me. I pulled back filled with indignation. To be asked a question like that. Why didn't he ask her?

"Oh, no. Have a donut, honey." He stammered. Donuts. Donuts. Not exactly my favorite food while on the Twiggy nutrition plan. I rolled my eyes.

"Where's the map?" Dad asked, gulping down a cup of the French Market coffee. His wheels were churning figuring out an itinerary for the day. He looked over at Mother. May as well make sure we're going in the right direction. No one wants to spend the day searching for the Astrodome." I happened to notice the bill for the quick stop groceries.

"Dad, uh... nineteen dollars and fifty-eight cents on cereal and juice? We could have all sat down in the restaurant and enjoyed eggs and bacon for that price!"

"Billy! What on earth did you get? We shouldn't have sugar in the car. We'll be dealing with ants." She said.

"What can you do? It seems we must be saving somehow. Kids are getting so smart lately, don't you think Butz?"

"Go pack, Marie Louise." Mother said.

"Tell them I said put their things out by the wagon. I'm about ready to load the top. And send Jimmy out on the double, Marie."

With doors and windows of the wagon shut, the world of the Guste's was an an ecosystem all its own. Our unique social order was governed by rules adopted and recorded in the journal of Monday night meetings held at home each week. Thanks to my novels, I could reach over into the real world outside the bubble. My parent's solutions to everything as well as their explanations began to be insufficient. I wondered how much of our religion represented successful indoctrination by previous generations. Aphorisms instead of answers, pithy sayings instead of engaging conversation were now insufficient. Were they trying to keep me quiet, make me mad, or actually provide a suggested philosophy? Their quick answers seemed like an effort to shelter me from truths about life which would eventually become obvious.

"Let's say a prayer and offer our day to God." Mother turned to smile at us. My inward reaction brought on immediate Catholic guilt. This was my mother. I adored Mother. Her ways of handling everything with grace fascinated me, her natural resilience and optimism were astounding.

"O Jesus, through the Immaculate Heart of Mary, I offer You all my prayers, works, joys and sufferings of this day...." She led us through the Morning Offering we were in the habit of reciting while en route to Sacred Heart every day.

"How about a song, gang? Let's have a round of Roll out the Barrel!"

After the warm-up, he called for his favorite "It's a Grand Old Flag."

"Butsie, please stick your arm out of that window to let that fellow know I want to get over." Mother complied, and a moment later Dad merged over into the middle lane. "I wonder how he knew what you wanted? I would never pay much attention to a woman's arm stuck out of a window myself."

"I've got a very special arm, then." Mom teased.

"Get the map open. I've got to pull over. Looks like we've passed up our exit.

It must have been that incredible show you all gave me, gang."

Inside the Astrodome, the sheer magnitude of the structure silenced the gang.

For a couple of minutes we stood still, tilting heads backward and faces upward, scanning the arched interior of the building. It seemed an unnatural wonder of the world.

"Amazing, Billy. Glad we came to see it after all!" Mom said.

"There's talk of building a domed stadium in New Orleans, Butsie. Now we know how great it would be, don't you think?" Dad said.

"Definitely. I've always loved football too. We ought to go home and talk it up." Mom replied.

The tour guide filled us in on a million way out facts and figures about the stadium – construction costs, shows coming to town, rain naturally occurring indoors, capacity, the history, employees and governance. Mother had her saddle oxfords on but nonetheless her feet began to hurt.

"Not too much farther, Ma'am. I think we've got our money's worth. This has been a nice little trek around these ramps. At least I wore my walking shoes."

Back in the wagon, Mother slipped off her orthopedic shoes and stretched her toes around. "Billy, there's one more thing we should see in Houston. It's the Warwick. I've heard it's a good hotel. Let's go by and peek. It might be good to know what the buzz is about. We may want to stay there next time."

"Great idea. How do we get there?" Dad asked.

"It's downtown near the Cathedral and the Museum." She said.

"I bet it's awful." Said Jimmy. "Do we have to go in there?"

"It'll only take a couple of minutes." Said Mom. "Promise. We'll just take a look at the Lobby.

While slipping on flat Capezio shoes she gave Dad directions. Mother had a nose for anything which was the quintessence of the good life. She knew exactly how the loveliest people would naturally do things, and that was the way she wished we would always do them. Her group was a work in progress. Where on earth did anyone learn all these minute details of social etiquette and manners and propriety? The rule book seemed endless. Was there a degree for this? She claimed it was her mother's training. That was Mima.

"Marie Louise and Melanie, you can wait in the wagon with the children. We'll only be a minute." Said Dad.

My parents returned shortly walking arm in arm, laughing as they looked at one another. As they pulled off, Dad winked at her mischievously.

Mother passed around a glossy postcard with a photo of the palatial lobby of the Warwick.

"I'm sure glad we stayed outside." Said Jimmy.

"I'm starved." Said Melanie.

"We've seen a lot this morning. Why don't we head back to the room and you all can take a swim. You can order hamburgers by the pool." Dad suggested.

"Sounds fine to me. I could take a nap." Mom smiled.

CHAPTER THREE

After the stop in Baton Rouge to meet with the Governor about the Charity Hospital Charter, we took off for Corpus Christi, Texas. Before long we were packed into two hotel rooms in the Hilton. Dad summoned me for a little father daughter time, pulling on some heavy black spit-shined shoes as he dressed for the opening luncheon of the National Housing Conference. "You want to know something, my creole tomato?" he said.

"Whoever heard of calling their daughter a tomato, Dad?" I balked and rolled my eyes. Being something to eat was bad enough, but a tomato? To him it was affectionate, because his mornings weren't complete without sliced creole tomatoes with his eggs. No matter how great tomatoes tasted, looked or saved your life, I felt it was a patronizing, disgusting put down to be called his tomato!

"Call me Daddy." he replied. Guess he thought I was still his little girl in light blue dresses and black patent leather shoes.

"Okay Daddy." I said.

"Listen, tomato, I'm so proud of you I can taste it!" Maybe he didn't hear my complaint about being his tomato. In one ear and out the other. "You're the greatest!" He sang the words with a cheerleader's zip and exaggeration.

"That's ridiculous Dad." I said.

"I couldn't be more serious. Mom and I are proud of you honey. You should know that." He was about to choke on his sentiments.

"Well alright then. Thanks." I said.

"You make the Honor Roll every quarter." If he was happy with my achievements why couldn't he just trust me more, ask me to do things rather than order me, let me go some and admit I was a sensible person. Why did he have to care so much about my grades?

"It's not such a big deal, Dad."

"You earned a blue ribbon for leadership, right?" The more enthusiasm Dad put into this, the worse I felt. What if I didn't do all this like he wanted? A little more spending money might have been a better reward. "It's a relief for your mother and I to be able to go out of town and leave the car keys with you, and everyone's streetcar and Coke money. We can trust you!"

"But you treat me like one of the kids. It's not fair." I said.

"You take time to teach C.C.D. on Sunday mornings to the crippled children." He said.

"It's my service work, Dad."

"And cheerleading Saturdays. A chip off the old block! A girl after my own heart!"

"I do for P.E. I'm nearsighted and clumsy so I never even try out for the sports teams. Coach Grenier lets me count cheerleading for P.E. credit. I admit I love it."

"And those dresses you've been sewing. How many girls your age do that?"

"Please Dad, stop. You've said enough, I promise!" I hated sewing my clothes but it was the only way to have anything besides my school uniforms and a Church dress or two.

"I can't help it, tomato. I'm proud of you."

"O.K. But please stop calling me a tomato. It's gross."

"Alright, tomato. I goofed." He pinched my cheek, then took off.

The road ahead of me seemed a little lonely. If Dad didn't hear me, how was he going to help me chart my course in life?

"Got any Jacks?" Elizabeth called out over the noise, stretched out on her tummy, propped on elbows carving holes in the plush carpet of a Hilton Hotel suite in Corpus Christi, Texas.

"Fish! Althea replied chuckling.

"Liar! You asked me for one a minute ago!" Liz popped back.

I marked the page in my copy of *The Grapes of Wrath* and fell into a snooze on the couch. From immersion in the western voyage of the Joad family, my dream landed me in the locker room at school yanking on gym shorts and wincing at the hysteria in the air over the morning headlines. America had invaded Cuba at the Bay of Pigs. My friends were sobbing. I moved quickly to get my uniform skirt hung and get out before catching the panic. Yanking on red sneakers, I gave myself a line about fear borrowed from Franklin D. Roosevelt. Oh no it was me now using the one-liners like my parents.

"This might be the start of World War III." Said Pam, the class worry wart. She wasn't the only Miss Doomsday today. It was almost everyone. Ouch. *"Come on, you all, is it that bad?"*

That morning at breakfast Dad had looked over the Times Picayune and stated the news about the Bay of Pigs in matter-of-fact terms, as if it were similar to other news stories we should be aware of. His tone was quieter and more restrained than usual. He said something about putting in a call to Mayor Vic Schiro and getting some Civil Defense courses going in the neighborhoods. He made notes on his legal pad. *"Oh for heaven's sake,"* I thought to myself, pitching my books on the floor of the closet and slamming the door shut. *"What's the use of worrying?"* I made my way past the mourners to the water fountain in the hall. The stream of water squirted high, splashing my face.

"Wake up, Mal." Althea prodded my arm. Back to reality.

Elizabeth came in the room looking angry. "Who took my combs? I just bought a whole pack and I can't find a single one. Althea, did you use them?" Althea threw her cards down.

"Say a prayer to St. Anthony, Elizabeth." Jimmy said with a mischievous grin.

"St Anthony? I won't bother St. Anthony with finding a ten cent comb! "Whoever took it give it over!"

"Maybe it was that Spanish maid, Liz." Althea called from the bathroom.

"Hmm. I noticed her eyes darting around the room pretty fast." Elizabeth replied.

"Elizabeth! Althea! That's horrible! She comes in here to give us extra towels and you lay blame on her. The poor thing. I bet everyone does that the minute they're missing something. It's prejudice. Do you even know what that means?" I said.

"I've heard of prejudice. It's white people who don't like black people, right?" Jimmy said.

"It means judging someone before you know them at all, and you base your judgement on their looks, their nationality, the color of their skin or some other characteristic. It doesn't only apply to whites and blacks. It's extremely ignorant and wrong."

"Un-Christian." Althea called out from the bathroom.

"Yeah. So don't let me hear any of you blaming the housekeeper again. It's atrocious." I picked up my book.

"Everyone's on my case again. They think I stole the combs. Mal, you know better." Althea looked mystified.

"Let's go for a walk down to Woolworth's, Allie." I said. "It's time we get a new set of cheap combs."

Built on a hillside at the edge of the Gulf of Mexico, Corpus Christi was filled with reminders that we were near a foreign country. Bright white adobe homes with red tile roofing and groups of black-haired children scantily clad running around in the streets. Strolling down to Main Street, I noticed their dresses and shorts hanging loosely from their slender brown bodies, and their adorable beguiling eyes looking up sweetly imploring. They grabbed my heart in short sentences in Spanish. The town was beautiful to me, named as it was for the body of Christ. People here were closer to the earth and the elements. They were spontaneous, honest and uncomplicated. There were sounds of music in the streets, aromas of every type and kind, a riot of colors everywhere. The foliage, the embroidered clothing, the pottery – all very pleasing to the senses. Earthy, warm, lively.

Mother must have loved something about it too. I remember that last day of the Housing Convention like it was yesterday. She was sprawled out on the king bed in her room waiting for Dad to show up, thumbing through a magazine, enjoying herself. After the meeting was over, Dad would be free for family fun doing some sightseeing. And she could enjoy all this closeness she cherished so much.

"Marie Louise, come in here and see something." She called to me. I quit packing and stepped into her room.

"Come take a look at this ad. There's a place in Mexico City where you can get priceless rings for a fraction of the price of the same rings here. Isn't this intriguing?" She said dreamily.

"So? It's all the way down in Mexico City, Mom. I don't know how much good that is going to do us. We're in Texas." I sensed there was a scheme brewing.

"Dad works too hard. Maybe we should convince him it would be educational to drive on down there and see the sights on the way to Mexico City."

"Do you know how far that is Mom? I asked her.

"How far is it?" she asked.

"Give me a minute. I'll ask at the desk." I told her.

As I went toward the door, she continued on. "It might be fun to take advantage of an opportunity while we're so close to the border. And these rings! What a souvenir. I love this blue topaz!" She said, holding up the newspaper ad. "It would be exciting." She jumped off the bed and circled around the room, fanning herself with the paper. "When was that meeting supposed to be over?"

I laughed out loud. "Mom, you want to drive all the way down there with this bunch just so you can shop the sales? Why don't we just find some sales around here?"

"I hadn't thought of that. We've had so many banquets and parties to go to. I wouldn't mind getting your father off somewhere where no one would know him, and ask him to do anything. To get him away from the conferences, clients, business calls, contracts, plans and pleadings to sign. To get him away from it all!"

"Yes, you could hide out in Mexico, with seven of your favorite children. Is that what you're thinking?" Again, I laughed at her playful plan.

Mother placed her right hand on her hip, and leaned her head to one side. A mysterious grin broke over her face as she looked me in the eye. The grin said "Watch me."

"You look exhausted, Billy. Let's get a rest before we go to the closing banquet tonight. Do you have a speech to give?" Mom said.

"Great idea, Butz. You kids, go to your room and get a book. We want some quiet for a while. No fooling around, just take a nap or read." Dad said.

After rest time, Dad sang out from the shower in his booming voice "My Wild Irish Rose." The aroma of French Market Coffee and

Chicory wafted in from their room. I cracked open the door separating the two rooms and breathed it in.

"Butz, I can't say this has been a real vacation. Ive been so busy with these meetings one after the next. You sure are a good sport, honey." He said.

"You know I'm proud of you, Billy. I think you need to get away from it all and take some real vacation time though. Give your mind a rest."

"You're right. I've been feeling it lately."

"It would be wonderful to get away somewhere where no one's going to call you about business. No meetings to go to. To be together for the fun of it." Mom strolled over to a spot behind the armchair to place her hands on his shoulders, then bent down to kiss his cheek."

"I'm in complete agreement. Were due for a break, big-time. I thought this would be one. Now they're expecting me back in the office on Monday." Dad answered.

"If you want to hear it, I had a brainstorm this afternoon – it's just an idea." And that's how it all started.

"We're so close to the border, Billy. When do we ever have the opportunity to bring the children to another country? Never! It'd be an education for all of us. Heck, I've never been to Mexico myself! It would be a ball. Call up Stella at the office and ask her to make some arrangements. It can't be that complicated. I know you can do it."

"The next day we went cruising toward the shore in search of a fabled local seafood restaurant called Flipo's and knew we had found it when we saw a huge concrete dolphin leaping in mid-air above the front door."

"This is it. Flipo's. I heard you can get good oysters in here."

A dark-haired man in a dirty apron opened the door just before my father turned the knob to let himself in. "Afternoon, sir. Restaurant's closed till supper. That'd be at six."

Dad stuck out his hand to shake. The man gingerly accepted. "I've heard lots about your cooking. Couldn't you make an exception and serve us some lunch? We won't make it complicated – just about six big oyster loaves and that'll do it. I'm dying for some good fried oysters – we're from New Orleans."

"Kitchen staff's already getting it ready for suppertime. When're they supposed to set up if they're serving constantly?" he asked, looking over the gang.

"At least they're still here! You could probably make them in your sleep from what I've heard. You've got a reputation that's pretty impressive, Mr. Flipo, is it?"

"Yep. I'm Flipo. Started this place thirty years ago. Hadn't had a free week since! People come down near the water and they want seafood. You got seafood, you got people." He was warming up, feeling proud now.

"Then you understand me. These kids are starved and as for me, I need some decent fried oysters, no kidding. You just don't get REAL food in those big hotels, Mr. Flipo. Come on, I know you can do it!"

"Okay then. Guess you can come in. We'll see what we can do." Flipo gave in with a chuckle and tousled Jimmy's hair as he slid through the door. Anne, Liz and Althea then crammed their way through at once.

"Girls, really!" Mother protested.

"Dad even admitted it. We're starved. Sorry, Mom."

"It's not as if you didn't have breakfast. Calm down." She said, indignant at the suggestion of hunger.

"Breakfast? I don't remember any breakfast." Althea said.

"Really! My dear child, you must have slept through it then." Mother flattened her skirt and looked around the room for the largest table.

"Right over here, Ma'am. Give me a hand sir, and we'll put two tables together right quick." Flipo rushed to help Mother and Dad deal with it. He showed himself a man with a good heart soon as we were inside. While the tables were being rearranged, I strolled around the room to take in the varieties of fish mounted here and there on the walls. As I stared up at the shark, my right foot crashed into a pail of soapy water and I suddenly found myself sprawled out on the floor drenched.

A sleepy waitress in a black and white uniform with a folded cap got up from underneath an open window and went for the mop, saying something in Spanish as she disappeared into the kitchen. Returning to the scene, she propped the mop near a table and adjusted her skirts, continually speaking to herself in Spanish. It sounded as if she were annoyed, and she acted as though we weren't there.

"Valerie's grabbing all the crackers! Stop it you pig! Leave some for someone else." Elizabeth fussed. The basket of Lance crackers was pulled apart by ten hands at once.

"Let's order immediately, Billy. Tell him to bring eight poor-boy sandwiches and a lot of French fries and that'll do it." Mother left for the ladies room quickly.

Flipo came and smiled mischievously at my father. He had taken off his apron and stood there inanely clutching at his suspenders with his thumbs, stretching them in and out. He had a receding hairline, black greasy hair, and a square shaped face. Behind horn rimmed spectacles his eyes gleamed. He pulled out a pad and pen and started writing.

"You want four seafood platters for this whole group. Okay, you say four we'll make four.

We'll do them extra large with some frog legs too. You all like tartar?"

"Oh sure, lots of it, too." Dad replied.

"And cokes for everyone, I suppose?" Flipo asked.

"Their mother doesn't let them have coke. How about lemonade or tea?"

"Okey-doke. You got it. Will that be it, sir?" he asked, apparently getting a charge out of the mayhem.

"Oh, and bring me a Budweiser quick if you can, Flipo."

"On the double, my friend. Just give me a minute. We'll get you all taken care of."

The air was salty and a warm breeze flowed through the wide windows along with afternoon sunlight. Flipo returned after submitting the order and pulled up a chair.

"You folks are the kind I like to serve. You really appreciate what we do here.

And you know something? You remind me of the days my wife and I used to take our children on trips in the station wagon, just like you're doing. Ours are grown now. We only had two, Mr. Guste. You got a big gang here, sir. Where you going next?"

"My wife and I are talking about a drive down to Mexico City. The kids have never been in a foreign country." My father replied.

"Brave idea." He looked around the table. "Mighty brave, I say. But anyways if you're just now thinking it over, my friend Sanborn across the street can tell you whatever you want to know. He's got the travel agency you go to if you're going down south of the border. It's his specialty."

"Hey, no kidding." My Mother returned and both men rose to seat her.

"Butz, there's a travel agency just across the street and they specialize in trips south of the border. How do you like that?" Dad smiled at her.

As platters were passed, Flipo hung around, amusement spilling from his face.

My father went on speaking with him while shuffling lemonades, catsup cups and tartar sauces. "My wife got up the idea the other day looking through the Sun Times.

You can probably give us some tips. I bet you've been down there a lot, living this close, right?"

"Tips? I could tell you about every square inch of Mexico, Mr. Guste. I know every cactus bush from here to Acapulco! It's been a favorite vacation of ours for years.

Good eating, souvenirs, good prices, too. You can't beat it!" Flipo went over to the front counter to get a toothpick and poured himself a cup of coffee behind the desk. He returned to give my parents notes for planning the next two weeks of my life. What a good heart the man had.

“Around these parts we’re excited about what’s going on out at Padre Island.

Say, Mr. Guste, has there been any coverage of the Island over your way?” Flipo queried.

“Don’t think I’ve heard a thing. You, Butz?” Dad replied.

“I don’t remember anything. What’s news?” Mom asked.

“You need to hear about it if you’re headed south. The atmosphere out on the island there, well it’s been compared to the Garden of Eden itself and mind you, they’ve started a couple of developments. It’s only one or two businesses managed to get a permit cause of all of them governmental rules and the environmentalists. One of my favorite customers is in the process of opening a new resort down there and it’s supposed to be the ritz. He’s aiming to please some real big time folks.” Flipo explained.

“Oh. Did he open up yet?”

“Truth is, I dunno for sure on that one. But it might be worth your while to find out if you’re headed down to the border. You could make a stop and get yourself all ready for the trip. He might run you some sort of special rate since he’s just about to take off, like an introductory special.”

“Good idea, Flipo.” Dad said.

"It might be hard to get a reservation if they're just opening up, don't you think?" Mom said.

"Don't worry about that. I've got some pull with the owner. Let me give them a call over there and see what the situation's like. He might have opened up just yesterday." Flipo took off for his telephone behind the counter. He picked up a business card from the Million Dollar and held it up in the air, catching Dad's eye.

"Wait in the car, kids." Dad said as he climbed out of the car at Sanborn's.

"Can't I come in Dad? I'm not really one of the kids, am I?" I pleaded. I knew he would be in there a half-hour at least.

"Stay and help. I don't want anyone giving Mother any trouble. Is that perfectly clear, gang? Practice your latest songs."

"Alright, if you say so." I resigned myself. I heard a round of groans from the rear of the vehicle.

"Don't be silly, kids. It gives us a chance to be together and get to know each other." Mom said.

"Get to know each other? Be together? Mom! We were just together at lunch. We've been together this whole trip." said Val impetuously. "Open that door, Althea, I need some fresh air bad."

"YOU need fresh air? Are you joking? You are the one with that disgusting B.O. stinking up this entire car! Do us a favor and try Arrid Extra Dry." Althea exclaimed in a high-pitched voice, fanning herself with a Mad Magazine.

"What about Dial? That's supposed to help." Jimmy piped up, chuckling.

"Eat your heart out, jealous!" Val opened the door at the same time climbing, practically falling out of it.

"Valerie, I'm ashamed of you. That's the whole point of a family trip – to be together, and be close. Besides, nothing in the world works better to make you appreciate home." Mama said.

"Ugh! Yes!" replied Valerie.

"Mom, do you want to hear a round of the song we sing when we're waiting for you?" I asked. It suddenly occurred to me that she might not have ever heard it.

"I'd rather say the Rosary." Mother pulled out the huge rosaries from the glove compartment. They were the ones from Rome, just like the beads the nuns wore hanging from their leather belts draped in a U-shape down the side of their floor-length gathered skirts. Father Romagosa had brought them back from one of his pilgrimages. Could people see into our vehicle, and if they saw, could they see our lips moving and tell we were chanting the Hail Mary, the Our Father, and the Glory Be? In Louisiana, we wouldn't exactly be misfits for this, but in other states, different story. They wouldn't take it as typical.

"Mom, doesn't it look odd the way when we're praying in the car? What do people think of us?" I asked.

"Nothing could be less important than what people think of us, sweetie. Now...."

"It's embarrassing. We need to pray, but can't we do it in private?" I implored.

"You'll get over that. If anyone notices us praying, it's good for them. Might remind them to do it themselves. Think of that. You're setting a good example."

"The First Glorious Mystery, the Birth of our Lord." Mom announced.

As much as I tried to discipline my mind to concentrate on the scenes from scripture I was supposed to meditate on, my mind drifted off from the Bible and floated away as I tipped my head to rest on the seat cushion.

Next thing in my mind was the image of my family seated for Sunday dinner, a ribald and festive mood filling the room. Dad gave everyone a turn to offer an idea or discovery from the week, an inspirational episode, or an incident involving an opportunity for service. You had to have something to contribute, no matter how trivial. Then in my dream state, came a beautiful image of my father's face welling up with tears of joy, lifting his glass of red wine over the group, searching across the long table for my mother's face.

"Okay, gang, I got all the information we'll need. Everything! Right here in this travel packet. It's the AAA of Mexico, can you believe?" "Maps, hotel and restaurant guides, road conditions, the works!"

Such a sudden burst of enthusiasm. Was this a thing decided? How? Oh my God!

"We don't have clothes, Mom." I said.

"All the more fun. No worrying about what to wear." She replied, giving me a big smile.

"Wait till the boys hear about this. Boy are they going to be jealous." Mel said.

Hear about what? What in the world is going on here? These people are acting as if there has been some sort of decision made about traveling in Mexico. How can you be having lunch one minute and the next minute you're mobilizing for travel to another country? Something's not right with this.

"They won't mind. They're proud to be working." Yeah, just what I wish I were doing. How did I get stuck doing this?. I am a hostage. "Those boys need some independence."

"What about girls?" I said.

"All in due time." She replied. "Billy, what about shots? Do we need to have any special shots to go into Mexico?"

"Did I hear someone say shots?" Elizabeth sprang into an upright position to participate. "Let's not go if we have to get shots."

"Scaredy cat." Jimmy punched her shoulder playfully.

"Pansy." Valerie called out.

"You baby." Althea added.

"Elizabeth! Scared of shots! Imagine – Best Camper at Skyline, best basketball player on the team, class president and scared of shots! Whew!"

"Scared of shots. No, I am not scared of shots. It's just that I hate shots.

It's not the same thing as being scared of them. I'm not scared of anything."

"Who is she kidding? What a joke!" said Val.

Mother looked over at Dad and gave him a smile. She spelled out these letters: I – G – N – O – R – E. She took a deep breath and lifted her chest as if proud of a secret trick.

"We must live right." Dad said, speeding up the Ford wagon heading out across the John F. Kennedy Memorial Causeway which led to Padre Island. This place was supposed to be like Eden itself, at least according to our new best friend, Mr. Flipo. Dad sure seemed in a hurry to step back to nature. I wasn't nearly as convinced.

I rested my head upon the window glass, tried to take in the sunset and ignore the conjecturing going on.

“Where is this place anyway?” Valerie asked.

“Not too far. We’re staying at the Million Dollar Inn. The name has a good ring to it. It’s supposed to be the ritz. From what I gather, it’s worth the drive.” Dad said.

“In that case, what’s this Coleman stove doing crowding up the back seat, Dad?” Val asked.

“They just opened up, but their restaurant isn’t in operation yet. So what? I usually don’t like hotel food. I like my own cooking, especially when it comes to steak.”

“The ritz! You call that the ritz, when you have to bring your own food and cook it?” Elizabeth called out.

“Shut up, creep. You know you can’t get a steak anywhere as good as Dad’s.”

Jimmy said. He hated sitting in restaurants with all the girls.

“Don’t say shut up again, do you hear me?” Mother gave Jimmy a hairy eyeball.

“I was just taking up for Dad.” he said.

“How far did you say this place was, Billy?” Mother asked. She stared out at a choppy Gulf of Mexico. From the size of the waves it looked as though there may be a hurricane forming out there. *The fun has just begun. Chaos. Is this the beginning of a bad dream, or what? I might have to begin talking to myself. I am going to go nuts.*

What is the phone number of Amnesty International?

“Isn’t there a grocery store on the island?” Mother wondered.

“It’ll be great, don’t start worrying. Anyway, what’s the use of worrying?” Dad said.

“This place must be in the middle of nowhere.” added Jim.

“Think positive, gang. You’re ALL PIONEERS!” He got revved up into the cheerleader persona.

Where did he get fixated on this pioneer imagery? Oh, yeah, from our slain President Kennedy’s Inaugural Address. It was the theme he used to define the era about a nation with a new frontier. And we were all the new pioneers.

“Like I said, think positive, gang.” There he went, the cheerleader. I spied a couple of signs posted on the railing indicating hazard. First, there was DANGER DEEP WATER. Then came NO SWIMMING. Then it was POLLUTED WATER. DANGER NO STOPPING. NO FISHING.

“Hey, when do we see the sign GO HOME?” Valerie asked.

"Perhaps it's time to think about that. Dad?" I asked gently.

"Gorgeous virgin wilderness. Remember those famous words of Flipo. Who has his telephone number?" Jimmy called.

Ten miles on the other side of the JFK Bridge I sensed silent unanimity.

"Commercially undeveloped property. Eden. Oh, now I get it. Look out there you all. All you see is a couple of lonely cactus bushes. What kind of hoax was this?" Melanie pieced the info together studiously.

"Just fantastic. How did we rate?" Valerie smirked. "Push over."

"It's lucky us, I guess." Said Elizabeth.

"Let's say the Rosary." Said Mom, popping open the glove compartment.

"No Butz, right now I need the map." Dad said.

"Billy, there is clearly only one road, and I did hear Flipo when he said it was a straight shot to the Million Dollar. Sounded good to me." My mother replied.

"I need that map." Daddy continued.

"Now I get it. They call it The Million Dollar Inn, because anyone who can find it can have the stupid million dollars." Jim let out a hoot. "We've been suckered in. It's a hoax. Boy, were we fools." He seemed to enjoy going on, stirring up trouble.

"You don't even think there is such a place?" Allie asked.

"Jimmy!" Mother was hot now. She cast him a dark look that told him to quit.

"Take a look around, Allie. You see anything out there? Rich people don't chase down this type of God-forsaken island. You'd have to be an idiot to set up a hotel in this desert. And crazy to go there, too." He kept going.

"Mother, Jimmy just said our family is crazy." Anne reported.

"We are headed there, Jim. Seriously, where is this place anyway?" I asked, leaning towards our fearless patriot. "Your pioneers are restless."

"Calm down you all, we're going to find it. Any minute now." Said Dad.

"Just tell us when. How about stopping at a Time Saver to ask directions?" Jimmy started up, the mischief shining from behind his tortoise shell frames.

"What Time Saver?" replied Dad, his face dropping. "I haven't seen a thing for miles?"

"Oh. No Time Saver or Pak-a-Sak? What is there then?

"I had an idea this would be awful." Said Allie.

"That's not positive thinking, sweetheart." Said Dad. If I had said what Althea said, he would've punished me. I'd never hear the end of it. Sweetheart? Unfairness goes around like a disease in this family.

"Mexico definitely doesn't sound any better, you all. What say we just change our minds now? Quit while we're ahead." Elizabeth contributed.

"It's about the shots, eh?" Val nudged her.

"Shut up." Liz said.

"Language off limits." Mother popped in, interrupting her work in the mirror.

"I get claustrophobia every time I hear the word Mexico. Don't use that word, okay everyone?" Valerie smushed her head against a pillow leaning on the window.

"If I've told you once, I've told you a thousand times, no one is to say shut up.

And Jimmy, I heard you take the name of the Lord in vain. Don't let that happen again."

Mother gave him a grisly stare.

"Where in the heck do we get directions? Can someone just tell me that?" Jimmy went on.

"Don't give in to worrying, Jim. It never changes anything." Mother answered him.

"You've got it, Butz! Give me a round of 'Pack up Your Troubles', gang!" Dad said, about to choke on his words. “I’ll bet we find that hotel by the time we finish it.”

Pack up your troubles in your old kit bag

And smile, smile, smile.

If you’ve a Lucifer to light your fag

Smile boys that’s the style.

What’s the use of worrying?

It never was worthwhile.

So. Pack up your troubles in your old kit bag

And smile, smile, smile.

Those indoctrinating lyrics! In my imagination I helped myself and traveled back to better days, like the day we rode in the citizen’s truck parade on Mardi Gras. In my mind’s eye I could see the kaleidoscope of colorful costumes in the street below us whirling around, and remember pitching trinkets and beads through the air. I remembered the sight of those arms raised like they were praying to us and shouting “Throw me something mister!” The horns, the bands, people hanging off their balconies with beers, the kids on ladders... I relived it all. I could almost smell the barbequed chicken, the hot dogs and hamburgers, almost feel the jerking motion of the truck moving forward after a stop. At the end of that crazy day, I saw a clown in the mirror with black streaks of mascara and dreamed of my boyfriend Mickey, the bearhug and the sweet kiss as we said goodbye. When my reverie was over, I felt like I had at the end of that Mardi Gras day, relunctantly returning to reality.

"Does that song solve a thing?" Jimmy asked. "I thought we would see the hotel as soon as the song was over."

Dad careened the wagon into the driveway of the Million Dollar. "Here we are!"

I looked out at a sprawling resort with sand-colored buildings cropped around in a semi-circle. It seemed like it'd be inviting once construction and landscaping were complete. I thought Flipo must be related to the owners or paid to get people here. Piles of rocks lay in piles here and there on the mud creating a desert ambiance. A bright green tractor stood by abandoned. At least it was a sign of man's presence.

"We didn't have any trouble finding a place to park, did we?" My father said, breaking the silence which had fallen over the wagon.

"Yeah, because there are no other cars anywhere around this joint." Said Elizabeth.
"Let's think positive." I said.

"That a girl, Marie." Dad popped.

"I told you anybody'd be crazy to come out here to spend time. I just knew it.

There's not a thing going on." Said Jim. "Whose idea was this anyway?"

"Jimmy keeps saying our family is crazy, Mother." Said Anne. My father began with a contrived laugh he forced himself to perform on occasions needing comic relief.

"Billy, stop that! It's ridiculous." Mother looked adamant.

"Hee, hee. Haw, haw. Ha ha ha!" Dad continued on.

"I said stop that this minute, Billy." Mother said in a low voice, about to growl.

"Butz, it's funny! You gotta laugh! It's the best medicine." Dad said.

"We know you're forcing yourself. It isn't funny at all. You were duped by that guy in the seafood joint. Construction isn't even finished. Look at that pile of rocks and sand. Hey, a bulldozer too!" Jimmy hooted.

"I see a beautiful stretch of beach. Look." Mother pointed west and the sun was going down.

"Hmm. I hope it doesn't rain tomorrow. I can get a tan." I said.

"The power of positive thinking." Mel quipped.

Dad returned to the car bristling with mischief. I had never thought of my father stopping off at a bar, but he was acting like it was a lucky day.

"Isn't this absolutely magnificent, Butz? I can't get over it. To think we'd never even heard of it! We sure are lucky to get in here tonight!" He exclaimed.

"What you're trying to say is, we couldn't have gotten in here last night, because it wasn't even open!" said Jimmy.

"That's my boy. I knew you had a good head on your shoulders." Dad said.

"You really mean it? This is their first night open?" I asked.

"You got it, Marie. They've opened up just for us. We are their first customers.

Just think, we're helping a family get a whole new business started."

"Exciting." Said Elizabeth.

In the room, I threw myself down on one of the double beds. It smelled like fresh paint in there. Dad pitched five tote bags on the floor at my feet.

"Help 'em unpack, tomato." He went in the other room, and started fixing a drink for Mother.

"Come on over here and give me a hand with this pit, Jimmy." Dad called over to our room. He appeared out on the sidewalk in a snap, his hair popping up frizzy.

"T.V.'s broken, y'all. Really great!" Val called out.

"Don't make a big deal out of nothing." Dad called out.

"You children must be tired. I'll call the desk about the T.V." Mother picked up the phone and dialed the manager. "Our television set needs a knob. Will you send someone over to fix it? Thank you." Clunk.

"Has anyone seen any toilet paper?" Anne called out in distress from the bathroom.

"Oh, just another Million Dollar blooper. No T. P. Ha! No food, no T.V. no toilet paper, no people. What a Million Dollar joke!" Jimmy crossed his arms.

"Aw, come off it, Jim. These folks have to start somewhere. It may as well be with us. Be a sport. I'm not raising softies." Said Dad.

"Yeah, Mom, I always wanted to go camping out." Said Val.

"Hello there, Miss. May we have two rolls of toilet paper?" Clunk.

"Tell them send a couple extra rolls for the midnight toilet paper party." Jim cracked.

A pubescent young boy white as a sheet turned up at the door, looking like someone was about to hit him on the back.

"Here's your paper, Ma'am. Sorry for the inconvenience. We're just getting started in this business."

"It's alright, son. Don't worry about us. How about looking into a knob for the television set. These guys would love to watch something while we get dinner on."

The timid red-haired youth cringed and his back arched upwards. He looked at Mother and stuttered, "Uh, oh, yeah, I mean yes, Ma'am, I was just about to explain to you. Uh, in just a couple of minutes we'll be able to fix that situation for you. Uh, see, no one can seem to find the knob and the house electrician isn't on hand at the moment. Soon as my brother gets here, I can move a new set in your room. We're real sorry about this Ma'am. We'll get it taken care of as fast as we can."

The new set was installed amidst cheers and laughs. Mother went into her room.

"Is that young man still around here?" She called.

"At your service, Ma'am. Anything you need?" He called back.

She came back in our room and looked the boy in the eye. "How about some hangers?"

"Your wish is my command." He said, saluting.

"You can set the table, now, fellows. This steak is just about ready." Dad announce from out on the sidewalk.

"Oh good, I'm starved. I'll be the one to test it. Just tell me when, Dad." Mel said.

"Just set the table while I slice it up. It looks "juste au point."" That was French for steak just at the point of perfection.

"Hey y'all, get this! No forks, knives or plates. Wow!" Val said.

Mother picked up the telephone again. "Listen, son, I don't mind being patient about the missing knob, missing toilet paper, missing coat hangars. But when my children are ready to sit down to dinner and feast on some barbequed steak to make up for all the surprises, does it have to be cold? Will you kindly hurry it up?" Clunk.

The fellow was there in a wink scrambling and cowering and stammering apologies.

"Hey, how about a rate reduction on these rooms?" Elizabeth called, as the guy disappeared out of sight.

Next morning I spotted that red-head guy kneeling in a future garden bed working with the valves in the filter system. People are so much alike, I thought. At home it was always my job to turn on the filters for the swimming pool in our backyard. He worked his way over to where I was sunning myself while he passed the vacuum.

"It sure is nice to see a family working together. You all have a gorgeous place. I'm sure it's going to turn into something spectacular." I said.

He lit up. "You think so?" He looked amazed.

"Sure. The beach is divine. And your hotel is super. Once you get all the details ironed out, it's going to be really busy around here." He kept going, smiling to himself.

"Mother, I need clothes to wear. I can't go out anywhere in these shorts and jeans." I complained.

"That's the fun of it. To be spontaneous and forget about planning what to wear. Just put on what you have. If anyone doesn't like the way you look, too bad."

"What if it's me that doesn't like the way I look? I don't like going around tacky." I said.

"Life isn't a big style show. We don't have to be dressed just right. We're in a foreign country anyway." This was new. Mom was always the one to care about manners, posture and the correct way of doing everything.

"Okay, Mother. If you say so. But I still think we are going to look tacky. We might even look like ugly Americans."

"Come on. It's your manners that count." She said.

Back in Corpus Christi, my Dad took care of getting Visas. It was coming into focus, a plan, that is, to travel South of the Border. All the way to Acapulco.

"It's countdown to take off. Pack up, guys. We're moving South." My Dad's instructions lowered like a hot air balloon coming out of the sky. This is really happening, oh my God, what am I going to do to get out of this. Maybe something will happen to make it fun. Who knows. Those rings were pretty, but really. This is going a little too far. What can my parents be thinking? How can they make me do this?

"The air conditioner always breaks down." Said Althea thoughtfully. "Remember that time in Texas? And the time on Skyline Drive? We thought we were going to die."

"What's the point of worrying. It won't change anything. Don't think about it." I said. The image of those fat colorful rings popped up on the screen of my brain. I'm sounding like Dad, and thinking like Mom. Chuckle. Life's ridiculous. What can you do?

"You can't tell me we're not overcrowded in that car. We ought to have two cars if nine people are going. It's cruel and unusual punishment, I say." Val whined. "I get claustrophobia just thinking about it."

"What's more, who says this old wagon can make it all the way? Remember all the car trouble we had last year on the trip to Grand Canyon?" Elizabeth conjectured. "What makes them think the same vehicle is going to make it through Mexico?"

"We'll deal with it as the situation arises." I said. "On a one-day-at-a-time basis, alright? To tell you the truth, I've never seen Mother and Dad in a mood quite like this. It might make for some fun." *What in the world is happening to me. I'm convincing myself of this. Norman V. Peale would be proud of me.*

"Yeah, don't waste your time worrying." Melanie said, folding her shorts.

"It never was worthwhile." Jimmy added with a long, long face.

"Y'all sound like Dad. I say the situation calls for some worrying." Valerie piped up. "I even heard Mother and Dad talking about bringing Kaopectate in case anyone gets diarrhea. I heard the food makes people sick. Terrific. I can hardly wait." Valerie crashed down on the bed.

It's not going to help anything if I encourage the negativism. I better stay positive. It'll have a ripple effect. We can make it fun, or we can make it worse. We better think positive. It might be survival.

Little did I know, I would shortly be in a steep learning curve. My eyes were about to be opened to the reality of the Third World.

"Don't let it get you down, Val. If it's bad, it'll count for some of your purgatory." I let out a laugh.

"That makes it better, Mal. Thanks a bunch." She stuck her head under the pillow and groaned.

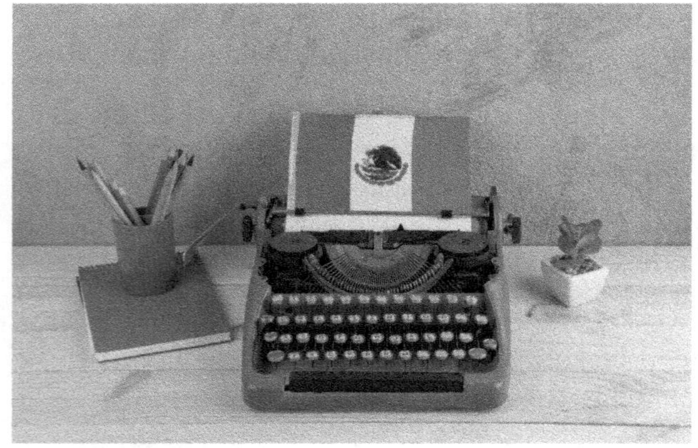

CHAPTER FOUR

The guys working the Mexican border patrol seemed way too gruff and angry at us. For no good reason too. They opened the tailgate, began to pop open suitcases and throw things around. It was a disgusting invasion of privacy.

"The guy's fiddling with Marie Louise's pink underwear!" Jimmy yelled.

"What?" I looked at him stony-faced. I straightened up and breathed deeply.

"Why the red face? There they go again. Here come the yellow ones. Yee-hah!" Jimmy continued.

I turned around to see three heavy-set black-haired customs officers rooting through my things. Midday heat sizzled. From their faces, you'd have thought someone was holding a leather bullwhip over them, telling them their pay depended on finding contraband. They puffed, panted and grunted asides to one another as they threw my things around.

I gritted my teeth. "Keep cool." I told myself. "Why let it get you?" Jimmy picked up my underwear and held them up. "Hey y'all, pink underwear! What a hoot!"

"A Mexican lingerie shower. It's raining underpants back there! Where did you get those, Mal? At the downtown Woolworth's or the one on Oak?" Melanie chided.

"Cheap skate!" said Elizabeth.

"Cheese ball!" came Melanie. "You'll fit in fine down South of the Border with that eye for color."

"Eat your heart out." I said, picking up my novel.

"If this is a lingerie shower where's the tea and cookies? I'm hungry."

Althea asked, sliding down on the floor of the wagon, flopping her head on the back seat.

"This is humiliating." Said Liz.

"Depersonalizing." I added.

"Disgusting." Anne added.

"Just plain gross. And where the heck's the bathroom?" Val asked.

The heat, the dry dust-laced air and three giant guys rooting through my stuff made me ill.

"They're searching us for cotton seeds, drugs or fresh fruit." Dad announced.

"Of all things! Us smuggling drugs? You must be kidding." Mom said.

"Couldn't they take our word for it, Billy? Do I look like the type to lie to anyone? This is positively absurd!" She went on, sitting up straighter. She pulled the visor down with a jerk, opened the glove compartment and grabbed the brush. After some rapid strokes out came the lipstick. "Doing this to a family on summer vacation.

Can't they tell we're nice people? This is going too far!"

"Perhaps they can't tell we are on a summer vacation. Not too many people cross the border with such a crowd in the car." Said Mel.

"We're suspicious one way or other." Said Dad. He smiled.

"We're nice people and it's outrageous." Said Mom.

Soon as one suitcase was slammed shut, they pulled down another.

"Look the other way." Said Mom, pressing her handkerchief to her face.

An hour later the chief inspection officer came out of the office in a navy blue double breasted suit and shoved some papers at my father through the front window.

"Sign here." He ordered, and looked the other way. He wiped his brow with a handkerchief. My father quietly looked around the back seat and caught my eye, raising his eyebrows. It had been a long time since anyone ordered him to do anything.

"Breathe deep, Billy. Don't let it get you." Mother cautioned him.

He signed quickly and started up the ignition. "Remember, gang, don't sweat the small stuff." He stepped out to tighten the straps and secure our things, then pulled off. It was unusually quiet for a while.

Moments later, Dad flipped the old switch to the sergeant revving up troop spirit.

"Just think, kids. In two short hours, we managed to travel to a different country.

No airplanes, trains, bus stations or terminals, no taxicabs, tips or hauling luggage!" He was himself again. A short wait in the customs office and we're here! Do you realize we are now in the country of Mexico? I hope it's the time of your lives."

"I have no doubt but we will." Melanie assured him.

"It's all part of a great education your Mom and Dad want to give you. No matter what it takes!"

"You mean no matter what it feels like?" I asked.

"Someone roll down the window!" said Val. "The air-condition isn't working."

"It never does in the middle of the day." Said Dad. "This is our gift to you kids – to see a part of the world that lies South of the border. We want you to learn as much as you can while you are here. You might pick up some Spanish, too."

"I bought the Berlitz guide to conversational Spanish." I said.

"Great! That's my girl!" he answered.

"Did anyone roll down the window?" Val said.

"I did but it's dusty out there and it smells." Said Jimmy. "I rolled it back up."

"Roll it down again. I'm suffocating." Val ordered him.

"Did you hear me? It smells out there." Jim continued.

"Maybe we're passing an oil refinery." Said Dad. "Marie, read me some of those expressions they give you for eating out in Mexico."

"How can anyone think about eating out? I have a stomachache and I have to go to the bathroom." Said Liz.

"Bathroom?" Said Dad, as if he had never heard the word. "Hmm. Don't worry.

We'll be stopping for gas shortly. Think of something else. Look out of the window."

"That's just what I'm doing. Funny thing, it sure does remind me of driving on Padre Island. Nothing to look at for miles around." Liz replied.

"There will be plenty to see. We're in Mexico." Dad said.

"All I can see out there is miles and miles of dry grass." She said.

"You have to wait. We're in the countryside. More of those expressions, Marie. Let's use the time."

"Muchacho means boy. All got that one? Jim?" I said.

"Where is the gas station?" Liz again.

"You mean 'estacionamiento'!" I said.

Mother reached for the black prayer beads. "Time for the Rosary."

Fifteen minutes later as the chanting drew to a close, Dad pulled up in front of two squatty tanks at a Pemex 100 filling station. "Just like it said in Sanborn's guide." Melanie cheered.

"Yeah. Did they mention this welcoming committee?" I asked, looking over at the road expert. Soon as Dad turned off the engine, seven or eight oversized men with dark hair wearing skimpy ribbed t-shirts revealing ample muscles surrounded the wagon as though this was a ceremony they had rehearsed. All of them had dark thick eyebrows like the customs officials. But these guys showed off hairy chests, and seemed to be glaring at us intently. They kept their arms crossed over their chests and stared at us.

"I've heard the people are friendly down here." Mel said. "But this takes the cake!"

"They don't have enough to do." Mom said, flipping out her compact.

"We must look like aliens to them." I said, and stuck my copy of *The Ugly American* in my purse.

"I could care less what we look like." Said Val. "But I can tell you one thing. THIS FREAKS ME OUT!" She said.

Dad played sergeant again. He put on a wide smile and looked around the back seat. Then turning to face forward he breathed deep, opened the door and stepped out. He stood straight and greeted each member of the committee with an eye-to-eye smile. I felt proud of Dad, always confident, always winning people over.

No reaction registered at all. They stared straight through him.

"Hello there, folks! We're here to get gas. You selling any today?" he asked.

The committee acted like they were glued to the ground and told to freeze. A young boy mysteriously scrambled out of the station office and began pumping gasoline into the tank.

"Good. Now. Who said they needed to go to the bathroom?" Dad asked, leaning into the vehicle.

"I did, Daddy. But I'm sorry to say – I'm scared to get out!" said Liz.

"That's O.K. I knew you didn't need to go that bad." He replied.

"Dad, uh...." Elizabeth stammered as she climbed over the seat and out of the wagon. "I do have to go!" she cried. Valerie and Anne sheepishly huddled beside her, and Dad escorted them to the back of the building.

When they were back, Mom spoke quietly. "I hope you didn't sit on the seat in there, girls. I forgot to remind you. And did you wash your hands well?"

"The soap looked like it was dunked in a mixture of scrambled eggs and mud." Val answered.

"Good. Then they're clean." Mom said, then gulped.

"It was disgusting in there!" Val reported. "There were lots of large flies and it was so stinky. I feel sick."

My father settled up with the cashier and got back in the saddle. "Mission accomplished, gang! We're on our way!" Jimmy and Anne popped into upright position.

"Boy am I glad that's over with. I was scared to death, Mom. I'm not going to the bathroom in this country. Those men all around our car stared straight at us. They were so mean." Said Anne.

"Is this what it's like to be in a different country, Dad?" asked Jim.

"No, son. That is what it's like to go to that particular gas station. Now let's hear a song. How about a round of 'Let the Sunshine In?' Ready? Let's hear it!"

Oh let the sunshine in, face it with a grin.

Smilers never lose, and frowners never win.

So let the sunshine in, face it with a grin,

Open up your heart and let the sunshine in!

"That was pretty good. But let me hear it louder, gang. One more time – now let's really hear it!" Dad said gesturing like a band captain.

"Billy, this is not a sound truck!" Said Mother indignantly. She rolled up her window, as if she might run into the neighbors and be embarrassed.

"Daddy, you know what to do about everything, don't you?" I said. My brother and sisters shouted the song to give Mother a time of it and watch. Wild laughter and hooting came from the back seat.

"I think those fellows back at the station could've done just about anything to us." Valerie observed. "That song was a relief."

"You see what I'm always telling you?" Dad said.

"Daddy, when are we going to get past Mexico?" Anne said, pretending innocence. Belly laughs and hollering again.

"She wants to know when we are going to pass Mexico. Pass Mexico! Get it? She's dumb." Jimmy squeezed out the words as he held his sides and bent over, wiping a tear from behind the glasses.

"Hysterical." Althea said, doubling over.

"Roll down the window." Valerie said, coming up for air.

"Yeah, past Mexico. Laugh all you want. It's time to go home." Anne said.

"You said that on the way out of Richmond Place?" Jimmy jibbed.

"I can't help it if I'm the one with brains." She answered.

"Anne! Think of the pioneers and it'll make it seem easy." Dad said.

"And never forget – it could be worse." Mother put in the famous adage.

"I bet it it'll get worse, too." Said Val.

"Time for a spin around the Rosary." Mother announced.

"Didn't we do that today?" Mel suggested.

"Some days you need two." Mom replied.

"Where's that map?" asked Dad. "I'd be glad to figure out where we are first."

"Where the heck is Monterrey is the question." I said. "There's no other road, so we must be on the right one."

"The man at Sanborn's assured me there would be no problem making it to Monterrey before dark. I guess we're not making good time since we stopped for gas." Dad said.

"Let's say the Rosary, Billy. I'm sure by the time we finish, we'll be there." Mom assured him.

"The single most important rule this guide emphasizes is that you shouldn't travel on the road at night. I've been studying Sanborn's." I said.

"I appreciate the input. But we don't need anymore of it, Marie." He answered.

"O.K. but be sure to watch out for stray cattle. And bandits who work at night. There's no sense being concerned about them, is there? What's the use of worrying? We're all pioneers!" I said.

Mother started in praying. "I believe in God, the Father Almighty...."

Things didn't look so good. But in spite of wanting to pray, my mind lifted off and took me back to our house on Richmond Place in the upstairs hall. It was night, and all my brothers and sisters were huddled on the floor on blankets. We each had a candle stuck on a green plastic plate, and used hurricane lamps to keep the flames going.

Three transistor radios kept us informed of the whereabouts of the deadly storm headed our way. It was Hurricane Betsy, and the eye of the storm was twenty miles away from the mouth of the Mississippi River. A Category 5 killer was moving toward us steadily. "It could be worse." My mother said. "Let's pray the Rosary." Jittery feelings of fear rose up inside me.

Soon the door of my parent's bedroom flew open and great gusts of air flowed into the hall. A siren-like sound came along with the force of 100 mile an hour winds. Dad was in the kitchen getting a jug of water we filled up with thirty others at 4 pm that afternoon. Large oak branches were crashing on cement outside while other tree limbs shattered the glass of upstairs windows on the front façade of the house. My head throbbed. I thanked God for the large white stucco house and worried about people who lived in little white clapboard houses close to water. My father returned with the water jug and Mother went to change the baby's diaper.

"Get some blankets, Billy. They're cold." He went immediately and pitched bedcovers at us from the girl's dormitory style room. Our legs were folded under us Indian-style on the floor in the candlelight. *Yes they are right. It could be worse. Thank you, God. There's danger out there, but we're mostly safe in here. We're all together. I know what love is.*

Another window in Mother's room blew as I heard the faint sound of Mom announcing the Second Mystery. In my dream, I watched the draperies flying about wildly like frenetic stallions unkempt manes.

"Close that door and get away from it." Dad ordered me. I heard toiletries and perfumes from Mom's dresser fly and shatter, then lamps crashing.

"It could be worse." I heard her faintly between Hail Mary's. My father shoved an armchair up against the door to their room to keep the violent gusts out. Flickering candles, slamming and shattering noises, wind blasts, and interminable shrill whistling all told us the killer was upon us. My brother's knee kept hitting mine during the rhythmic whispering of prayers – it all combined into a faith sceance. Moments like that never leave you, they define you. My daydreams were telling me we were headed into an experience which would cement bonds of family.

I returned to the station wagon, lost in the mountains on the road to Monterrey, Mexico. Twilight fell and the western sky – a palette of mauves and greys and blues beckoned me into a dreamlike feeling. The mystical palette painted itself on my soul.

Dusk fell into night. Moments later, a galaxy of flickering lights appeared on the horizon. It was the city of Monterrey. "Look, you all. I see it. It's got to be Monterrey!" I called out.

"Hallelulia, brother." Shouted Jimmy.

"At last!" Valerie chimed in.

"Pull yourselves together." Mother said.

Jubilant frenzy gave way to quiet attentiveness as Dad whirled onto the main drag of the city. Every face found a window to nuzzle up against as eight passengers perched for an experience of the unknown. An entirely different civilization–Mexican. Sights, sounds, smells and colors all worked a mesmerizing effect and a respectful hush hovered over the troop. There was much to take in at once, all of it unusual and strange. Exotic and inviting. Colored lights hung across the streets, romantic music flowed from small sidewalk cafes, little children scampered around barefoot in front of their parent's curio shops, sides of beef hung in open air markets, stocky dark butchers stood at attention in white aprons ready to slice. Enchilada and taco vendors displayed their wares in the streets. Ladies with bushy, shiny hair cascading down their light brown backs attracted customers into shops, their lacy wide gathered skirts flowing around in the night air to create rainbows of bright color. Sights converged into a welcoming kaleidoscope. The earthy quality of it all brought thoughts of Steinbeck's novels. It was colorful, interesting, different from anything I had ever seen. Romantic. A little dangerous and mysterious. Perspiration dampened people who shined of life. Jovial and playful ladies bristled with vitality as their little boys chased each other around. Their husky daddies seemed resigned and exhausted.

"Where's the hotel. Who has directions?" Dad asked. "Marie, pull out the book! There was supposed to be a sign on the way into town."

"We missed it, then. I'm just thrilled to roll into something resembling civilization again." Mom said. "Find that guidebook back there."

"Roll down the window and ask, Dad. I'm getting hungry." Said Elizabeth.

Dad stuck his head out at the next red light. "The Ramada Inn?" He called out to a pedestrian.

"No comprendo, senor."

"Get serious. There's nothing to comprendo. They don't like us." Val griped.

"And the guide says they're so friendly." Said Liz.

"Hey, there's a person who looks relaxed on that corner. Ask him." Mel suggested.

"The Ramada? Si Senor." The young man pointed and gesticulated and Dad pointed and gesticulated back, smiling. Progress! I loved it when Dad would make a friend this way. The man finally waved, called out adios, and gave a big smile. Dad swerved the vehicle into a one-eighty and headed up a mountain road that curved in and out.

"Hey, a sign over there says The Ramada!" Valerie shouted.

"Thank God." I said. I looked up at a dazzling sight – a majestic Ramada presiding over the side of the mountain and keeping her watch over the city.

"Lord, thank you! It looks lovely." Mother choked up with relief.

It was a sprawling three-story structure with Spanish accents. The cream-colored stucco façade wrapped in chocolate railings was warmed with golden light pouring from iron lanterns gracing each balcony. Homey magnificence. Splendid for the occasion.

"I'm tickled to death we found a nice clean Ramada." Mom went on.

"Who says it's clean?" Said Jim.

"You may not realize it, but this is a Mexican hotel." Said Mel. "It's as Mexican as any other hotel down here. It's part of an American chain, but a Mexican bought the franchise. That ought to make everyone happy." Melanie had been reading Sanborn's.

"This is important. Listen to me, children. DON'T DRINK THE TAP WATER. Did everyone hear me?" Mother said.

"We hear you. Promise." Jimmy said.

"Don't drink any water from the tap for the next two weeks. Do you understand?" Mom repeated.

"Honestly, Mom, we get it." Called Valerie.

"Everyone I spoke to about travel in Mexico emphasized that we would get sick to our stomachs if we swallow a drop of that tap water. Did everyone understand?" She kept drumming it in.

"Cross my heart hope to die. We understand. Promise, Mom." Melanie reassured her.

"We'll get something to drink in the restaurant. You won't die of thirst."

Grabbing two tote bags, I climbed out over Allie who was sleeping on the floor.

"Allie is out like a light. Get up, Allie, we're here." Liz shook her. "Come on, we found the hotel. You're going to love it. Oh, and Mom said not to drink any water. It makes you sick."

"What?" Said Allie, rubbing eyes. "Oh, it's pretty."

"Just don't drink any water when you go in." Said Liz, leaping out with totes.

"But I'm so thirsty!" She climbed out of the car and the daze.

The well-dressed valet showed up promptly.

"Have you folks got a cot or two for the small kids?" Dad made eye contact and smiled.

"No comprendo, Senor." The fellow looked apologetic.

"You know, amigo, a big bed, like this." He opened his arms as though to frame a bed, lifted it, then walked his imaginary creation over to the existing double and plopped it down, pretending it was heavy. Feigning slumber, he rested folded hands near his cheek, closing his eyes and painting sweet dreams on his face.

"You know, senor, a bed!" He said assuming eye contact again. He pointed to the existing beds as if trying to poke a huge hole in a piñata.

"Two." He held two fingers up, like this was going to be it. "Two more beds!"

"No comprendo, Senor." That one again.

"No comprendo? I just explained it to you!" My father was speaking to the boy as if he were his own stubborn child. "I guess I've got to call the manager. Butz, let's freshen up quick and we'll go down for dinner. I'll discuss it with the manager in the lobby. I can communicate with just about anyone!"

"It didn't work with the bellboy." Said Mom.

"I can communicate with anyone no matter what language they speak!

All you have to do is get eye contact and add some gestures. Got me through the war in

Europe." Dad ignored her comment about the bellboy.

"What was the matter with the bellboy's ears?" She queried.

"He didn't want to go and get rollaways. A little lazy. Probably came to work today and will quit tomorrow. He's just a kid, but he didn't want to understand!" Dad went on.

"I get it now." Mom put on lipstick. "It's a relief to me to know we have one person in our group who can communicate under any circumstances." She popped out the pressed powder compact. "Now I know when we get lost, it won't be for long." She winked over at him.

"Most people love to be helpful. They'll make an effort. And if they don't understand, they'll find you someone who does." He settled into the plush armchair and smiled, noticing the landscape through the window.

"I feel safe with that." She went over to knead his shoulders. She smiled and leaned down to get eye contact. He pinched her cheek. "Maybe the manager speaks English. If you start the mime routine, we might get an audience." She suggested.

"Don't be ridiculous. And please don't worry about the looks of things."

"Someone has to be." She went to the door. "Children, pull yourselves together.

Wash your hands, comb your hair and tuck those shirts in. We're going down to dinner in a minute. It's an elegant restaurant too, so please be on your best behavior."

Althea combed her hair near the bathroom mirror, and then turned on the water to wash her hands. She cupped her hands to take a few sips of water and then proceeded to wash her hands. She had been fast asleep during Mother's drill about not drinking the tap water. "Don't drink that!" Elizabeth hollered from across the room.

"Allie, did you drink some of that polluted water? Oh my God!" I exclaimed.

"Marie, don't use the name of the Lord in vain. Ever. What's this about anyway?" Mom asked.

"Althea took a sip of the water" I said.

"Stop making a mountain out of a mole hill. She just took a few sips. They probably meant if you drink a glass of water it'll make you sick. Think positive. You can force yourself to get sick if you think negative. Out of this door, this minute. Everybody!"

Downstairs, Dad refrained from dancing around and dramatizing to get the beds and the younger kids were too tired and hungry for acting up. In the dining room, large round tables surrounded a grand fountain which was lit up and danced with prismatic colors of the rainbow. Three musicians strolled around in sequined costumes under a canopied courtyard, visiting tables.

Mother made a fuss over selecting a table. One was too close to the bathroom, one too near the corner or the aisle, another near the kitchen door where the waiters might spill things on us, another in a drafty area. Dad and the waiter patiently attended her as she chose the perfectly appointed table.

"I suppose this one will do." She finally made her choice. I wondered if she did this to enjoy seeing how accommodating her husband was. Dad made sure she had the perfect table and Mom was of course pleased as punch.

"Let's see what they're cooking up and get in our order. I'm convinced I have every kind of blood in me." Dad said.

"What do you suggest for dinner, Billy?" Mom asked.

"First let's get the waiter." He signaled. The caballero popped over. "Guacamole salad. We'll start with that." The waiter nodded and Dad returned to thoughtful reading of the menu.

"Yecch." Jimmy blurted out.

"May as well try it all. It's bound to be good. How about two taco dinners, two beef enchiladas, two cheese enchiladas, two burritos." Dad continued as the waiter scribbled it all down. "What about for my first lady, Butsie? We should try the Chateaubriand"

"Fine with me. I be glad to try that." Mom replied, closing her menu.

"Can we get some crackers? I'm starved." Val said.

"O.K. gang, let's hear what's on your mind. Everyone take a turn and say what they're thinking about. If you're thinking, that is." Dad started up the round table.

"When do we pass Mexico? I asked today, but no one answered me." Anne feigned innocence.

"You didn't notice everyone laughing at you?" Althea asked gingerly.

"The answer is—in about two weeks." Dad replied.

"Aw, rats." She pouted.

"That's enough from the peanut gallery. How about some input from some of you Marie and Mel? What's on your mind?"

"I'm reading all of Ayn Rand's books this summer. She's a fanatic on the subject of American individualism. Her philosophy is exciting." Melanie said.

"What's exciting about it?" Dad asked.

"I am a rugged individual at heart. I can't stand all the conformity I see around me." She looked straight at me. "It's sad the way unthinking people adapt their lives to style, and worry with what other people think."

"I don't have a gripe with being stylish, Mel. And I don't worry about what other people are thinking about me."

"Why do you have to be stylish to have a good view of your self?"

"You don't even seem to know what the styles are. Are you really trying to play like a tom-boy? Or maybe a revolutionary, the way you wear those cut-off blue jeans and act like it's cool."

"Are you criticizing my cut-offs now?" She passed me an icy stare.

"And those high-top tennis shoes with shorts! What are you trying to say to the world?" She acted as though she had no idea that I thought of her clothes as a statement.

"What's your gripe? I happen to like baseball. Cheryl Tiegs wouldn't approve?" Tiegs was a cover girl for Teen Magazine.

"I like baseball too. Nothing's wrong with that. I play less now that Mom and Dad allowed me to go on dates. It doesn't hurt to look good and it takes time to sew things to wear." "Teen Magazine isn't so bad. At least you get an idea of what the styles are."

"I hate that garbage. You pretend to be intelligent, yet you voluntarily allow yourself to be drawn to things they dream up on Madison Avenue. You'll buy any style even if you look bad in it. Those magazines prey upon insecure people and make them buy stuff they don't need. It galls me to think Mom and Dad consider you smart!"

"I guess you told me." I said.

"No offense intended. It's constructive criticism. You're a conformist." Mel went on.

"This started out a philosophical discussion, girls. It's getting too personal." Dad broke in.

"Personal? That's an understatement! I didn't even know she thought about me like this!" I exclaimed.

"Don't be oversensitive, tomato. Your turn. What's on your mind today?"

"You want the truth?" I asked.

"I want the truth." He said.

"It's about the way you force us to go to Mass every day." I said.

"Force?" He asked.

"I'm sixteen now. It's not that I don't like Mass. I don't want to hurt your feelings. I just don't like the way you force us into this regimen, and don't give us a choice." I wondered how I got that out. My stomach tightened up.

"Whoever said anything about force?" He asked innocently.

"What do you call it, then, the way we just go? No one ever even mentions the fact they might not want to. We're too scared to say so." I wondered to myself if this is what happens when you travel in a foreign country.

"You mean you don't want to go to Mass and offer you day to God, tomato?"

"Dad, I've told you this before, and I wish you would listen. I am not something to eat. Now. About your question. I think it's wonderful to go to Mass. It's just that at my age, there ought to be a choice. Sometimes I need more sleep. I've got a lot of extra curriculars. You say you're proud of that." I said.

"I am proud of it. Ideally speaking you may be right." Dad admitted.

"Aren't you the one in favor of living by ideals? What gives?" I continued.

"You probably should have a choice. And I bet you'd make the right one every time."

"Interesting form of persuasion."

"You're the leader among your sisters. I need you to lead the way for your younger brother and sisters."

I felt even more trapped. He isn't just making me go, he's getting me to lead everyone else. There didn't seem to be any way out. "If you get a willy-nilly attitude or get lazy, it'll rub off on them right away. Don't you understand, Marie?"

"The boys aren't forced to go. They're older than me. Why aren't you worried about what example they're giving me?" I argued.

"They have to get to school earlier than you. And it's across town. They get breakfast over there." He said.

"Please pin yourself down. Now that we've had this discussion, and everyone has aired their viewpoints, do I have to go or not?"

"I never said you were forced to go." He artfully set his emotional trap once again.

"No, not really." I answered. "But why is it we all just go?"

"Did I ever say you were forced to go?" He asked.

"Not really. I didn't even know I could ask about this. That's how regimented you have us."

"The results look good to me. You are doing well in everything."

"So bottom line is – I do have choice." I stated.

"It's really the best choice you can make, the best choice in the world when you have the opportunity. To go to Mass and Communion every single day. Nothing is more important." He explained, avoiding my question once again. I gave up on him. At least I had been able to say what I thought. That'd have to do for now. When I looked over to Mom for support, I could tell something was going wrong. There was a look of shock on her face. She stared at Allie, upright in her chair. Allie was white as an alabaster statue.

"Althea, what is it honey?" Mother begged, getting up and rushing around to Allie's side. "You look sick."

"Butsie, it's been a long day. Althea's pale all the time." Dad said.

"She looks like she's about to faint." Mother took Althea by the shoulders. "Honey, what is it?"

"My stomach. It's killing me. I'm really, really sick." She slumped into Mother's arms.

"Did someone say Althea had a sip of the water upstairs? I told you all not to drink that tap water." Mom said.

"Althea was asleep when you drilled us on it. I tried to tell her when she woke up." Liz explained.

"My stomach is going to explode." Said Allie, looking whiter and more aghast by the minute. Dad got up, came around, picked her up out of the chair and carried her to the bathroom, with Mother trailing beside them. When Dad returned to the table there was a mood of gravity.

"Must be horrible." Anne said. "She looked white as a sheet."

"Good she didn't pass out. Looked like she was just about to." Mel said.

"It must be that bug." I said.

"What bug?" Valerie asked.

"The bug. In Mexico, "the bug" is diarrhea. You get it if you drink the water from the tap. That's why Mom was telling you not to drink the water. Now you get it." I explained.

"Yeah, Miss Know-it-All." Val said, stuffing a chunk of sourdough bread slathered with butter into her mouth.

"Quit stuffing your face with that dough, Valerie. There's only so much room in the middle seat for all of us. You're the one with claustrophobia. What happens to the rest of us?" I said.

"That's just superstition what you all said about a bug." Said Jim.

"You can decide after you have a touch of it. See for yourself." Mel said.

"I'm really scared." He said, buttering his crackers with a gleam in the eyes.

"Alright, kiddos, they told us not to drink the water. They warn you for good reason, so let's not question it. There's no reason to press our luck and find out the hard way. Just don't drink the tap water! Everyone acknowledge."

"Yes, sir." Came the response in unison. When he spoke that way we knew to sit up a little straighter.

Mother and Allie returned to the table quietly. No one said anything for a couple of minutes. Althea sat on Mother' lap for the rest of the meal.

ALL THIS CLOSENESS

CHAPTER FIVE

"Out of that bed!" I called, yanking sheets off them one by one.

"You're not even packed up. Get going!"

"Shut up." Jimmy called, flinging his Superboy comic book in my direction. Dad appeared and grabbed him.

"Follow me this way, son. Double-time, please." He ordered.

"I'm hardly awake. I've got to pack." Jimmy protested.

"Just follow me, my friend. Take this bag in one hand and this one in another. And tuck this guide book under your arm. Let's see those muscles." He urged.

"Dad, uh really." Jim acted dopey.

"We're the men in this situation. I'm counting on you. Follow me." Dad picked up a couple of bags and ambled down the stairs.

"Hey, I'm only eight you know. These girls are a lot older than me. They can help too, can't they? Anyway, don't they have bellboys in this hotel?"

"Why waste a minute bothering with that fellow they sent us last night? I need to be on the road before noon." Dad huffed.

"What?" Jimmy asked.

"I need capable help. Like you." Dad said.

"Okay then. I'm strong."

"I'm glad to have a son along!" Dad gave him a pop on the back and began pitching suitcases on the luggage rack.

"Thanks, Dad, but I don't see why the girls can't help. Are they sick? You've heard Melanie talking about Women's Lib. She says women can do anything men can do. Why can't she help you load the car?" Jimmy asked.

"You've got a point there, Jim. I'll get her help next time." Dad winked at him.

Melanie and I showed up to clear gum wrappers, checkers, crumbs, cups, plastic forks while Dad and Jim continued with suitcases, canvas, ropes.

"Mal says she women can do anything men do. Ask her to do something that takes a little lifting and she can't. That's a man's job! Ha!" Jimmy called out.

"I didn't say I couldn't do it, Jimmy. I can haul and load suitcases, but I don't mind there being jobs that men just do. Like that one." I said.

"Sure. Try and get yourself out of that one, smarty." Jimmy chuckled.

All this closeness! I looked forward to a different closeness in which someone hear me and understand, love me for me.

“Did any of you drink the tap water in the bedroom this morning?” Mother asked.

“No way.” Valerie said. “I’m not getting that bug.”

“Anyone else?” Mother polled the troop.

“No, Mom.” One after the next came the assurances.

“Allie was extremely ill last night. Let that be a lesson. Don’t drink that water. Do you hear me?” Mother continued.

“What about brushing our teeth, Mom? May I use tap water? Elizabeth asked.

“Good question. Billy, can they brush their teeth with the water?”

“Where’s the map?” Dad called out over the discussions.

“About brushing teeth. I need an answer.” Mom pressed on.

“Oh, that.... Of course, don’t be ridiculous. They have to brush their teeth, don’t they? Just don’t swallow any water when you rinse your mouth.” Dad coached.

“There’s bottled water, Daddy.” Jimmy said.

"Bottled water? No, just don't swallow any of that tap water and you'll be fine. Swish it around, spit out and you're done. Not a big deal." He explained.

"Sounds impossible to me. I'm not brushing my teeth." Althea stated.

"Thinking about brushing my teeth without swallowing makes me choke." I said.

"Mexico! How did we get into this mess anyway?" Jimmy asked.

Mother passed him a dark glance and he slumped down in the seat to avoid her.

"I might not mind driving through Mexico, but when do we pass it?" That became her refrain to spark a round of belly laughs.

Mother straightened up and breathed deeply. She pulled down the visor to check her face, applied lipstick, then went for the Rosary beads.

"Come on, Butz. Be honest. It's a new experience for us." Dad said. "Let's have a round of 'Oh Suzannah'"

Oh, I come from Alabama with a
banjo on my knee,

And I'm bound for Looziana there
my true love for to see.

Mom turned to Dad for eye-contact and placed her hand on his shoulder. Giving a wan smile, she held Althea a little closer to her.

"Come on, Mom. We love Mexico. It's great! It is exciting to be in a completely different country. No meetings or banquets. Just time to be together! Remember?" I said.

"I asked for the map a while back. Now find it! And I mean now!"

"Oh no. Where is that thing?" I said, pushing aside people's feet and other gear stashed behind the driver's seat. "I saw it a minute ago."

"Where?" said Dad, raising the volume just a tad.

"We're going to find it Dad. Give us a minute. We're looking. Promise." Said Mel.

"It's one thing to drive to Mexico City with a map. It's a completely different thing trying it without your map close by. I don't want to go ten minutes without that map. What if we run out of gas in the middle of nowhere?" He warned.

"We don't want to either." I pictured having to pee behind a cactus plant.

"Pray to St. Anthony." Mother chimed in. "Better yet, offer him a dollar if we find the map. St. Anthony..." She began addressing him in person. "I'll put a dollar in the Poor Box if you help us find that map."

"Found it!" Called Liz. "Do I get the dollar?"

"I said 'in the Poor Box', Liz. Pass the map forward, please." Mom said.

"But I'm poor as can be. Basketball doesn't pay."

"Liz, you don't have any idea what poverty is. You've never missed a meal." Mom explained.

"I don't have a red cent. That's not poverty? Someone stole my last quarter out of my pants." She griped.

"Maybe the maid in Corpus Christi, Liz." Jim pricked the bleeding hearts.

"Think it was Valerie? She pulled your shorts on in Houston?" Said Althea.

"Althea is making that up. She's the most suspicious one in this family. Always disappearing behind curtains and chairs with something she shouldn't have." Valerie suggested.

"I always tell the truth." Said Allie. "I must look suspicious to people. Everyone looks at me when something's missing. No fair."

"It's your eyes, Allie." I explained matter-of-factly.

Dad pulled over to study the map. "Sanborn's makes it all look so simple. Trouble is, I don't see one sign along the road to tell me where the heck I'm going."

"There's only one road to drive on. There are no exits." I said.

"You don't see too many intersecting interstates, do you?" Liz laughed.

"Just a couple of intersected cactus bushes!" Valerie added.

"We're in the middle of nowhere." Said Jim.

"What's the use of worrying?" Elizabeth reminded him.

"That's the spirit, Liz! Let's hear it, gang. It never hurts. Come on:

Pack up your troubles in your old kit bag, and smile, smile, smile.

If you've a Lucifer to light your fag, smile boys that's the style.

What's the use of worrying? It never was worthwhile.

So! Pack up your troubles in your old kit bag and smile, smile, smile.

"Now, Dad," I said, leaning my chin to rest on the front seat. "May I help with that map?"

"I'm looking for a place called the Hacienda Chicken. Sanborn's says there's a palatial mansion outside a town on the road to Quanajuato. We ought to stop there for lunch." Dad said.

“The Hassee end of what?” Jim let out a hoot.

“The Hacienda, that’s ha-cee-end-ah, chicken. Easy. Try it, Jim. You’ll be speaking Spanish.” Dad said.

“Ha-cee-end-ah Chicken.” He called out.

“Bravo!” Dad cheered him as he returned to the map. “There’s no education in the world quite like travel in a different country. Look. Jimmy’s speaking Spanish!”

“It’s especially great if you can find where you are.” Said Mel.

“I’m getting hungry.” Said Val.

“I have to go to the bathroom.” Said Liz. “Plus, I could use some fresh air. Roll down the window. Even if it does smell funny out there. The air conditioner doesn’t work too well. It’s 11:30.”

“If we just move forward, there’s bound to be a gas station where we can ask.”

Dad said, starting up the ignition. A few minutes later he pulled up at a Pemex station.

“I never thought it could be a relief to see a Pemex station.” I said.

“You said a mouthful. Maybe this one isn’t as bad.” Val said, climbing out of the car door the minute the vehicle came to a halt.

"Get back in this car immediately, Valerie. We can wait till we get to the restaurant. The bathroom in there will be nicer. We need to be careful." Mom said.

"Nicer bathroom. Mom, I've got to go! You haven't been to the bathroom at Camp Maryhill in a while, Mom. They stink too." She whined.

"If it's such an emergency, go on. But don't sit on that toilet seat." She said.

"God-in-heaven, it smells awful in there!" Liz exclaimed, wide-eyed.

Mother looked like she'd been shot in the back with a stun gun.

"Where on earth did you find such a hideous expression?" Mother asked. "I have told you all I won't tolerate any of you taking the name of the Lord in vain." Mother looked at Elizabeth intently.

"It's hot around here. I'm sorry, Mom, really. I won't say it again. But I can't even describe how it smelled in there. If only we didn't have to go to the bathroom in Mexico." She said.

"I told you to wait and go at the restaurant. Gas stations are like that." Mom said.

"Yeah, first we can stop brushing our teeth, then we can stop going to the bathroom. What next?" Jim hooted.

"Oh, fun!" Anne popped.

"My suggestion was to go at the restaurant." Mom said.

"I'm on the right track. Think positive. We'll be there in a couple of minutes." Dad sang out.

"A positive thinking lesson coming." Jim said.

"Smile and the world smiles with you. Frown and you frown alone." Dad sang those words proudly, plastering on the big smile.

"You know how to deal with everything. That's for sure." I said to Dad.

"I do my best." He acknowledged, shrugging.

"Looks like home on the range again. Remember Padre Island?" Jimmy reminded me.

"One round of "Home on the Range", and we'll be there. Let's hear it:

> *O give me a home where the buffalos roam*
>
> *And the deer and the antelope play;*
>
> *Where seldom is heard a discouraging word*
>
> *And the skies are not cloudy and gray.*

"Are we there yet? You said we'd be there if we sang it." Jim complained.

"That was super. You're good musicians—like the Trapp Family. Time for 'I've been workin' on the Railroad?'

I've been working on the railroad
all the livelong day.

I've been working on the railroad,
just to pass the time away.

Can't you hear the whistle blowing, rise up so early in the morn.

Can't you hear the whistle blowing, Dinah blow your horn.

"Dad, you sure we're on the right road? We're hungry." Jim complained.

"Sure as anyone could be. The guy at the gas station explained the directions."

"In perfect Spanish?" I asked.

"I'll get you there. It's a promise." Dad chuckled.

"I have to go to the bathroom." Val admitted sheepishly.

"You just went." Said Mel, incredulous.

"Valerie has diarrhea!" Jimmy said.

"I do not." Val said.

"We could start the Rosary." Mother suggested.

"Butz, save it for after lunch. We'll be there any minute." Dad said.

"Say a prayer to St. Anthony everyone." Mother replied, still holding Althea.

It appeared like a mirage – a palace on the plain, and it was all it was cracked up to be. Dad pulled to a stop and a hush dropped over the troop like a tablecloth being lowered gracefully on a table. The sight of this mansion was a little mesmerizing after the drive through the plains. I clutched my Berlitz guide to conversational Spanish, and reached for my purse.

"What're we doing sitting here?" Liz exclaimed. "Let's pile out!"

She climbed out in a huff. "Hey, this looks alright with me!"

"Three cheers for Sanborn's." Allie added.

"And one for the driver." Mom put in, looking for Dad's eyes. "This place looks fit for a king."

"And for a queen." He approached to offer his arm, and they led the way in to our oasis for the day.

Our luck – we were the only patrons to be on hand just before closing time for lunch. The maitre-d'hotel stiffened his gait as he led us to a lengthy table near the picture window overlooking the vast, warm and desert-like countryside.

"Tell him the glare is too strong over here. Have him put two tables together in the middle of the dining room." Mother said.

Dad waved down the waiter with confidence. A stony, snobby guy came back and the maitre-d complied with help from one of his underlings. Dad joined in moving chairs and received non-verbal communication that his assistance wasn't welcome.

"I know I can communicate in any language, Butsie. All you do is try to make contact. You people settle down and get comfortable. I'll go and use the facilities." Dad said.

I settled down to open the menu. Pages upon pages filled the leather-bound volume. Certain words popped out which could be understood readily. As to the preparation details, there was no hope.

Dad returned in high spirits and dressed in a new chalky moustache.

"You should've waited fellows. It's mighty clean in there." Dad's amusement was running high.

"Do you mind if I ask you a personal question, Dad?" I asked.

"Depends on what it is, tomato." He answered.

"What is that white stuff all around your mouth?" I said, suppressing a laugh.

He didn't seem to be aware he was wearing the new beard.

"Oh!" He dabbed the lower half of his face with his napkin, as if someone caught him in the act doing something he shouldn't. "Guess I forgot to wipe my face in there."

"Whatever you did in there gave you a moustache." I told him.

He leaned over. "I thought I'd take a little Kaopectate as preventative medicine." He indicated by way of a facial expression that I was to keep this between us.

"Dad took Kaopectate in the bathroom!" Jimmy announced confidently.

Dad threw him a warning immediately and a round of giggles ensued. Once again, he pressed the napkin around his mouth. The giggles turned to hysterical fits of laughter.

Anne got a red face. Melanie choked and took a sip of water. Dad didn't like it much.

"What are you doing taking Kaopectate in the bathroom?" Liz asked. "Is it a new cocktail?"

"Actually, no! Would I drink a cocktail in the bathroom before lunch?"

"Sometimes you do it in the hotel room, Dad." Liz answered. Dad looked at Mom for help. She looked at her menu.

"You didn't tell us you were sick." Liz went on.

"Sick? I am as healthy as an ox." Dad replied.

"Then what are you doing taking medicine when you don't need it?" Althea asked innocently. "You always tell us not to take medicine unless you're really sick?"

"Alright I should explain. This is preventive medicine. I'm the driver so I need to make sure I don't get sick!" Dad explained.

"I know you aren't sick! You'd never get sick, would you? You have the bug! That isn't sick when you're a traveler in Mexico." Val concluded.

"You're right. And if I would happen to have a little stomach ache, I wouldn't call that sick, either." He went on.

"Dad has diarrhea." Jimmy told us. The laughing started up, and Dad's face became red.

"Billy, laugh at yourself. You're always telling them they'll never get anywhere in life if they don't do that. Now just give it up and laugh. There's nothing wrong with getting the bug!"

Dad smiled and gave in. "All I can say is don't tell me what I'm having for lunch. I plan to have it all. Let's order."

"We'll have a platter of enchiladas for the children. I'll take the guacamole and tacos. How about the perfect steak, Butz? It's their strong point."

"I'd love that. Won't you have some too?" She replied

"I'm going Mexican. In this five-star place you'll get the best."

Althea sipped her coke and nibbled oversized fluffy crackers. Her color returned slowly.

"I'm going to the bathroom." Val announced. "Anyone want to come?"

"Again? Didn't you go at the gas station?" Mel inquired.

"Valerie has diarrhea, just like Dad and Allie." Jimmy stated.

"Jimmy! Please." Mother said looking around at the elegant interior of the Hacienda, and then over at the waiters. "Let's call it the bug from now on. It sounds a little nicer."

"Alright. Promise. It's the bug from now on." I said.

"Now that it's settled – Valerie has the bug. Ha!" Jimmy said, and raised a toast.

"I do not have the bug. I don't even get sick. Did you forget? I've had only one glass of water and one coke so I've got to go to the bathroom."

Back at the wheel with all the cartoon characters aboard, jabbering, yacking and arguing over their regular places and turns, Dad stretched his arms and took a long slow breath as if to say get ready, get set and go. He turned to his troop, the future leaders of society, and to the peanut gallery.

"Is the gang all here?" He beamed, and gave that nod of the forehead which blended courage and diplomacy. The nod meant he expected an acknowledgement.

"All hear!" Came the cry in unison, effort being made to give him what he expected – a sound of enthusiasm.

"Ready to brave the wilds, Dad. We've got a good meal to go on. And some hope too." I said.

"Is everybody happy?" Boomed the cheerleader, with his right hand for a megaphone.

"Billy, please." Said Mom.

"Well, yes." Came a dull response.

"I didn't hear that, gang. Let's hear it." He tried again.

"Well yes!" Came overcompensated assurance from the home team.

"Jimmy slumped down on the mat and got grouchy. "Oh no, here we go again.

How long will it be this time, six hours?" He complained.

"I've always told you, Jimmy – 'it could be worse.'" Mother smiled at him fondly. Her cherished tools made for a good life, and when life was tough, they made it possible. These adages were riches to Mom. "It could be worse." She closed her eyes and contented herself.

On the road again the sergeant waxed philosophical and pretty quickly it appeared as though it may crank up to a full-blown lecture on endurance. Nothing anyone hadn't heard a whole lot about, mind you.

"Smile and the world smiles with you, frown and you frown alone. Children, your mother and I love you, but we didn't have you for the fun of it. We want to make men out of you!"

"Billy! Of all things to say. It's mostly the girls this time. Please!" Mom protested.

"They know what I mean. I want to raise leaders—people with character and lots of it. Courage and spunk. Stict-to-it-tive-ness. Drive..."

"Enough said, Billy." Mother stammered, pulling down the visor.

"We know what you mean, Dad. And we understand. We're behind the program." I hoped to shorten the speech.

"But I need to drill it in. You may have heard it a whole lot but Liz, and Jimmy and Anne are just arriving at the age of being able to fully get it." He said.

"I won Best Camper last year, Dad." Liz defended herself. "People look up to me."

"Then you younger guys back there. I don't care whether you're a boy or a girl it shouldn't make a difference. I want you to live by principles and strive for greatness. Yes, greatness." He continued, beaming.

"How do you know if you've achieved it or not?" I asked.

"You never rest on your laurels no matter what you achieve. You always strive to do your best in everything, even the things you're not naturally talented in. If you take music, and it's not your best subject, do the very best you can. Don't miss an opportunity. You may not finish first, but you learned a lot and you might have contributed something, too."

"I'd rather concentrate on the things I am good at." I said.

"When you have a choice, fine. Sometimes in life you have to do things that you don't even want to, or that you didn't picture yourself doing. That's where a positive attitude comes in. You adapt. And not only that, you strive to be cheerful about it.

You become a good team player."

"I don't like ball sports because I'm not good at them." I said.

"You can still enjoy playing the game. And if you've got the right attitude you never know, you might be needed for something." He said.

"Sometimes we need an extra player just to play in the tournament." Liz said.

"I get it." I said.

"There's strength in numbers. Remember that, you people." Dad went on.

"I was following your drift, but where did that come from." Melanie asked.

"A team of individuals can accomplish so much more together than they could've ever achieved alone. That is, if every one cooperates and follows a leader. I want to make a team out of you. And not only that, a team of leaders."

"It's okay to be on a team of leaders, but don't try to make a man out of me." I said. "I'm fine as is."

"That's not what I mean, and you know it. I want to see strength, courage, and and a generous spirit of helping out where you're needed." He said.

"We've been through this before." I said.

"We need to go through it over and over. It's so important. Now more than ever." He said.

"Yeah, because we're going on a survival adventure on the roads of Mexico?" Jimmy asked.

"Possibly." Dad admitted. "You don't know what you'll meet up with from day to day, but if you have character and confidence you can meet any situation in life head on. And if you've got a team, well, there's nothing you can't do!"

"I can think of a few things." Jimmy said.

"You know what I'm talking about."

"This is beginning to get depressing." I said. "It's not the smells in the air or the dust. I'm almost used to that. I just don't think there is an easy answer to everything. Couldn't you admit that?" I told him.

"Out with it. What's the big problem?"

"I'm beginning to see that half the world considers us 'the ugly Americans.' I began. "Didn't you feel the disdain of those waiters? So nasty and stiff. You've never been treated like that anywhere. And don't tell me you haven't noticed the workers at those Pemex stations. Even the owners were cold to you. You're the friendliest guy on earth, Dad. That's got to be an attitude towards Americans."

"That book you referred to, 'The Ugly American', did you read it for a course?" Dad asked.

"For social studies." I said.

"Did you learn to worry from the book?" He asked.

"It made me worry. The world's problems are unsolvable. What a mess we're in, to tell you the truth. There's hardly a thing anyone can do about it. And it keeps on getting worse." I said.

"You can't take that approach. You just have to try to help where you can, and encourage others to do the same. If everyone does what they can, things improve." He said.

"I hope you're right. The book says that the image of Americans in many countries of the world is that of over-fed, noisy, obnoxious people. They think we're rich, insensitive and selfish." I said.

"Even more of a reason to travel in this country. We need to let people here know that Americans are okay." Dad said.

"All we need to do is show a good attitude and we'll be doing something for international relations." Mom said.

"It gets me upset when I realize there are people in the world who live hungry." I said.

"What good is it going to do to get upset? Roll up your sleeves, reach out and do whatever you can to help. Then live with a clean conscience." He said.

"I wouldn't be a Christian if I didn't worry about it. I don't want some easy answer, Dad." I said.

"This is not my easy answer. The answer I give you calls for action. It's weak to worry about something and do nothing about it. It is strength to be concerned and to act on that concern." He explained.

"What if I had been born in different circumstances? Let's say in a slum. Would I be singing spirituals or causing trouble on the street? I don't even know. Maybe I wouldn't have faith in God either. Who really knows? Maybe I believe in God because I'm one of the lucky ones. What's fair about all this?"

"Life isn't fair. Leaders who care try to do something about it. If you were born in difficult circumstances, I believe you'd be the same wonderful young person you are to us. God loves you, that's all." Dad said.

"I'm not sure about all this. How could God let things get this way – totally unfair. It makes me feel guilt."

"Guilt and worry are closely related. Neither one does you any good."

"Maybe not." I thought out loud.

"You control guilt and worry. They'll bog you down. And keep you from action that helps the situation. Getting depressed is a waste of time. Act on your concerns. I'm proud of you for thinking about it all, honey. It's good to think, but it's important to direct your thoughts wisely. You can't work things out by brooding too much." He said.

"Yes, sweetie, don't let it get you." Mother said.

"What's the use of worrying?" Mel quipped, smiling.

"It never was worthwhile." Val popped.

"Water off a duck's back." Allie added.

"Take it with a grain of salt, Mal." Jim mimicked Mother.

"Smile and the world smiles with you..." Liz threw in her suggestion.

"Is someone trying to make light of this? It's serious." I said.

"Don't even talk about getting depressed. That's not the spirit. Keep your chin up, Marie. It's a responsibility. You can't live for yourself. You need a good attitude if you're going to do anything to help the world's people!"

"Me, change the world. Fat chance! I don't think there's a single thing I can do which would really make a difference." I said.

"Now you're talking about hopelessness and defeatism. Is that courage? Confidence? Leadership? I don't think so. You need to act on hope. We aren't going to solve it all in one day, young lady." He said.

"True." Mom said. "So let's offer our Rosary for all these intentions. You have to turn some of these things over to God, and let Him tell you what to do."

She reached in the glove compartment.

"This is something we have to wrap up, Butsie. Let's at least finish the conversation." Dad requested. "Now tell me, Marie, have we gotten anywhere understanding each other?"

"Yes. But why doesn't it seem to worry you at all? You're so optimistic it's unreal. It seems you'd worry about it at least some, because poverty in the world is upsetting." I said.

"Marie Louise! Your father would take the shirt off his back for someone who needed it. You know that! He does so much for others, I couldn't stop him if I tried." Mother protested.

"I'm sorry if it sounds like I don't realize it. You do lots of good things, Dad.

I know that and I try to do everything I can too, I promise."

Mom started in on the Rosary and I conked out asleep. Before long the dreaming had me going from one apartment to the next in the Iberville Project bringing Thanksgiving baskets around. In the dream he hauled a huge basket up a flight of steps, set it down in front of the door and pulled a comb out of his back pocket to tidy up his appearance. Inside the humble, state-subsidized dwelling, Dad would accept a Coke, sit down at the kitchen table and make friends. He spoke about any topic that would come up and if nothing came up, he'd think something up. He had a way with people. He always made them smile and laugh, and truly enjoyed knowing them. He listened to their concerns. He didn't mind if they showed up at his door from time to time, either, even if it was during the Christmas party. He kept a few gifts aside in case one of his old friends from the project showed up Christmas day. Then my dream took me to the Orphan's Christmas party in the gymnasium of Wright High School. Dad organized it all, introduced Santa, and called the children grade by grade to come forward and receive the gift Papa Noel would hand them. Next in my dream came a scene where I was playing around with the energetic pre-school kids at the Jackson Barracks after Hurricane Betsy. Our school Headmistress had called me to come over to school during our days out of school to help out with the kids housed in the barracks after Hurricane Betsy. How adorable they were! How much they seemed to teach me. Mother's voice broke in on my dream imaging.

"The Third Mystery, the Birth of our Lord. Let's offer this mystery for the intentions of those who are suffering or hungry, and ask the Lord in His wisdom to show us the way to help." The faint sound of her prayers came through.

I woke up in that white Ford station wagon full of kids zooming along a quiet road searching for a town called Quanajuato, Mexico.

ALL THIS CLOSENESS

CHAPTER SIX

"Is this Guanajuato?" I said, fumbling around for Sanborn's guide and the map.

"No, it's 3:30. An hour and a half to go. Get me that map back there—on the double!" Dad rolled the window down and leaned his curly head out. "You know the way to Wano Wano?" he shouted to a young boy on his bicycle in the street.

"Please roll up the window this minute" Mother winced, flicking the visor down to tidy her hair. She shook her head, and ran fingers through her hair.

"Dad, it's Guanajuato. 'Waa-toe'. Not Wano wano!" Mel said. There came the hooting and hollering.

Sticking his neck back in the car, Dad shot a look signaling they better sober up.

"Keep it down in here, I'm trying to get directions!" Out went his head again.

"Billy!" She almost choked, making sure not to raise her voice. No use, he didn't hear a thing.

"Where's Wano Wano?" He shouted loudly, but the boy looked back with a blank expression and remained silent.

"You're asking directions from a small child." Mother tried again.

"Let's pull over and study the map." Mom suggested, the whites of her eyes bulging with horror at Dad's misbehavior. Dad pulled to a stop on the edge of town. A giggle escaped from Anne, and she ducked. Jimmy crouched down and held his mouth.

"Daddy, it's not Wano Wano. It's Guanajuato." Said Val.

"Who taught you all this, young lady?" he inquired.

"Marie. She read us the history of the castle at Guanajuato from that guide."

"Okay. You people be quiet when I'm asking for directions."

"We can figure it out with the map." Mom looked him in the eyes. A giggle escaped from Anne. It got contagious.

"Dad, you look funny leaning out of the moving car with your curly hair yelling 'Wano Wano' at the poor boy!" said Mel gently.

"You tell us to laugh at ourselves, right?" I put in. His face softened.

"Yeah, practice what you preach, Dad!" said Jim. Dad stiffened again and looked back. Jim ducked out of view. "Oops. I didn't mean it like that, Dad. Sorry." Dad started with his canned laughter, hooting and hee-hawing in a crazy sort of way. Mom pulled out her fan.

The wagon emerged from the little village to face a long stretch of two-lane blacktop ahead.

"How many miles, Dad?" By then it seemed like the world's stupidest question.

There was quiet.

"At least we know where we're going." said Melanie, with the map in her hand.

"Dad, how many more miles?" Liz asked pretending it was a new question.

"We'll see."

"That just doesn't work! It's an easy question."

"I tell you 'we'll see' when I don't know."

"Okay, but what about an estimate?" She persisted.

"Look. Lunch was a feast. Now's our chance to be together as a family and see the beautiful country of Mexico. What's the hurry?" Mother said.

"I don't see what there is to look at in Mexico. We've been on the road for miles and miles and I'm sick of it!" Val explained.

"And you can't roll the windows down because it smells gross!" Said Jim. "It smells like someone's passing gas every minute of the day!" Said Jim.

"Allie was sick. It must be her." Valerie said.

"Valerie is trying to pass it off on Althea! She has diarrhea!" shouted Jim.

"The bug, Jimmy. Remember?" Mom said getting eye-contact.

"Valerie has the bug!" Jim reaffirmed.

"You can't roll down the window in Mexico! At least on this road anyway. It's like breathing in dust. It's hot too!" exclaimed Val, the whites of her eyes brightening. She blew air into her mouth and her face puffed up into a rotund ball.

"Grouch!" Jim announced.

"Shut up, you two, I'm reading the map." I said exasperated.

"I told you all don't say 'shut up'. That'll be a fifty-word composition about the correct use of the English language!"

"Okay, Mom. Sorry. Pipe down, guys. I'm to figuring out arrival time." They leaned their heads in my direction.

"What's it say, Marie?" Said Liz.

"Just a minute and I'll tell you." I declared, studying the situation confidently. We have about an hour and a half's drive left." I announced.

"My God, I can't take it that long!" exclaimed Val, bewildered at the prospect.

"That'll be a fifty-word composition, Valerie." Mother said.

"Sorry, Mom. I don't believe I can take another hour and a half of being jammed in here like sardines. There's nothing to look at on the road. I'm bored."

"How did we get into this anyway?" Said Jim.

"Valerie." Dad said. "It's part of a great education I want to give you. You would never realize what a wonderful country we live in, if you never traveled outside of it!"

"There's no McDonald's, no Stuckey's, no billboards on the road, hardly any sign of life on the road. We're in the middle of nowhere." Val went on.

"I've been feeling a lot of love for our country lately, too, Val. Let's have a round of "God Bless America!" said Dad.

God bless America

Land that I love

Stand beside her and guide her

Through the night with the light from above.

From the mountains, to the prairies,

To the ocean white with foam.

God bless America, my home sweet home.

The gang belted it out more fervently than Dad expected. He turned to look at us with Irish eyes.

"Keep your eyes on the road, Billy." Said Mother.

"I've never felt this much love for America in all my life." said Val.

"Me neither." Said Jimmy.

"That's the beauty of it, children. You're finding out how blessed you are! There's no better way to find that out!" said Dad, wiping a tear from his eye.

"It's a great opportunity to be together." Said Mom. "Being together for two weeks helps you get to know each other, and sweat each other out!"

"All this closeness is good for us, right Mom?" I asked her.

"You know what I mean!" she said glowing like queen for a day.

Val twisted her rear end around to try to budge Melanie over.

"When you're stuck together you're forced to learn to practice teamwork, and get along!" Said Mother.

"I have it the worst!" said Jim. "I need to get along with six girls!" he said.

"You're feeling sorry for yourselves. If we didn't need to think about Montezuma's Revenge, I'd give you a good dose of Milk of Magnesia!" said Mom. "People get grouchy when they need a good cleaning out."

"Don't talk about Milk of Magnesia, Butsie. I'm about out of Kaopectate." Dad replied.

"I guess it wouldn't be good in Mexico. But I always say, if you feel grumpy, maybe your system needs a purge. If we were in the States, I'd look for a fruit stand and give you each a good piece of fruit. That'd help!"

"That's just it. We're not in the United States. And it's getting to me." Said Liz.

"Don't let it get you. If all else fails always remember – it could be worse!" said Mom. I was getting tired of maxims.

"If you don't think it could be worse then think of a situation that would be worse. You'll start to count your blessings." Said Mom.

"What could be worse than this, Mom? I've had it!" said Val.

"We might never have found the Hacienda. Then we'd be starved!"

"Let's hear a round of 'You're a Grand Old Flag'" Boomed Dad. "I've never been so filled with love for my country!" "Come on gang. One. Two. Three:

It's a grand old flag, it's a high-
flying flag

And forever o'er the free may it wave!

It's the emblem of the one I love

The home of the free and the brave.

Every heart beats true for the red white and blue

Where there's never a boast or brag.

Should auld acquaintance be forgot

Keep your eye on the grand old flag!

"What a sound. You don't know how happy you've made me!" He turned back to glow with love and pride.

"Keep your eye on the road, Billy!" Mom said.

"Let's hear it for a Yankee Doodle Dandy!" I imagined red, white, and blue balloons rising into a clear blue sky, and a Marine Corps Brass Band striking up a half-time show.

Oh, I'm a Yankee Doodle Dandy!

A Yankee Doodle do or die.

I'm a real live nephew of my Uncle Sam

Born on the fourth of July.

I've got a Yankee Doodle sweetheart

She's my Yankee Doodle joy.

Oh Yankee Doodle went to London

Riding on a pony

I am that Yankee Doodle boy!

"That was beyond belief kids! Butz, we've got an army here! I can't tell you how grateful I am to you! Y-O-U! My Butsie-Boo! We can change the world for the better. You know what, kids? All this traveling reminds me of my time in the Army." Mother folded her arms in front of her and looked out of the window.

"I was supposed to be in the infantry, but I had flat feet so they put me in the cavalry." He reminisced. "I was stationed in France during the Second World War."

"I doubt you were serving during the First World War! You're not that old!" I said.

"Tell us about that gorgeous blond girlfriend again." Said Jimmy, checking Mother's face.

Mom straightened up. "Haven't we heard these stories 1,000 times, Billy?"

"I never get tired of them, Butz. It's an education for the kids to hear what it means to be ready to fight for your country!"

"Let's hear about the girl-friend." Jimmy requested once again.

"You mean June?" Dad asked.

"Enough is enough!" Mother said.

Dad laughed, reaching over to pinch her cheek. "Butz, you know I've never loved any one the way I love you. Do you people know you have the greatest Mother in the whole world? And I have the greatest wife in the whole world!"

"Calm down, Billy." Mother flipped the visor down and applied lipstick. "Would anyone like a mint?" she said pulling Cryst-O-Mints out of her purse. "These won't last long, but at least everyone can have one." She passed them around. "Let's get some more in Guanajuato."

"Tell us about the olden times in the Army, Dad. C'mon." Said Jim.

"O.K. I was getting around to telling you about my days in the Infantry before they switched me out. Talk about making men out of you! No one can serve their country if they can't take the heat. You've got to be a man, have courage. You can't be a ninny and think you're going to do anything to serve your country and your fellow man. That's why this trip is the greatest thing on earth for you, kids. I want to make men out of you!"

"Cut that out, Billy." Mother asked. "You mean make good people out of them."

"Mom's right. I never intend to join the Army anyway!" I said.

"Ah ha! You don't want to serve in the Army, but you think women can do everything that men do—and just as well. Baloney! You're a ninny, and a big fake, too."

"I can serve in the Army, Jimmy. But I don't plan to!" I explained.

"Marie, I want to make men out of all of you," said Dad. "And I mean it! I want to raise you to be people with character, ready to fight for your ideals and for your country!" exclaimed Dad.

"Maybe I'll join the WAC's one day. Who knows? I guess I could handle it."

"You know this country wasn't built by softies, Marie Louise!" said Dad.

"What country?" I asked.

"The United States of America!" he hounded.

"We're in Mexico." I replied.

"Oh, Marie Louise, you know what I mean!"

"I know what you mean."

"The pioneers who built our country had courage, faith hope and love. They had the determination to build a country that would offer a better life for all inside its borders. We're still building that country. We're all pioneers, working to make their dream come true!"

"It's the best country in the world already. It's a free society. America is the most powerful industrial nation in the world." I said.

"But we have yet to make the promise of liberty and justice for all come true." He said. "We need to wipe out poverty, unemployment, illiteracy, hunger and social injustice within our society!" For Dad, it wasn't just talk. He threw himself into every effort in sight, and started initiatives right and left. His life was poured into making the dream come true for all.

Mother said reaching for the prayer beads. "Time for the Rosary!"

"The Rosary, hmm..." Jim lay down immediately.

"Why not a song?" said Liz.

"The Rosary." Mom repeated, handing the beads around.

"I say a nap" Althea put in.

"Maybe a presentation on Model Cities!" I said.

"It could be worse!" said Mom, shaking her head. "In the Name of the Father, and of the Son...."

Fifteen minutes and the quiet chanting worked. Five out of seven travelers were fast asleep, with Melanie and I hanging in there for prayer time. At twilight we wound our way along a narrow mountainside road. A truck approached on one of the sharp turns and Dad stopped the car.

"Whew." He looked out over the side of the mountains, and took a deep breath. "The sun is going down, Butsie."

"Don't remind me." Said Mom looking back.

Melanie and I burst into laughter. "Out on a winding mountain road at night in Mexico. This is a bad introduction to life in a different country!" I chuckled nervously in response to fears envisioned – more trucks, maybe bandits, more narrow curves at a treacherous height. Giggling turned into uncontrollable laughs. Mom's face became stony.

"You girls are acting like you're Jimmy's age. This is no laughing matter!"

"I know it isn't funny, Mom, but I just couldn't help it." Mel explained. "First we drive all day on two-lane highways with nothing to do but try to convince ourselves we're not lost. Now we're on a mountain drive with the sun going down and it doesn't seem safe! Things are going from bad to worse!" She explained.

"Butsie, you're always saying 'It could be worse.' Now take it with a grain of salt. We'll be there in a while." Dad said, starting up the car again. Mother turned to give a look of censure.

"Oh Mother, please." I begged. "Remember how you're always telling us not to make faces? We don't mean any harm. We're just getting punchy. Laughter is the best medicine!" The more Mom wanted to suppress it, the funnier it seemed.

"Butz, we're on the right track. If it'll make you feel better we can say the Rosary again." Dad tried to console her.

"We just finished the Rosary! That's enough! Please!" I protested.

"We might need it. Did you see that truck?" Dad said. He started praying.

Mel and I tried not to laugh, but it kept getting funnier. By the time we reached the "Glory Be", we broke out cackling. Mother interrupted the praying.

"I can't believe this immaturity, Billy. Two grown girls acting like two-year olds! What do we do? I'm floored!"

"We're sorry, Mom. We're feeling a little scared, too, and it's getting us punchy." I said. A tear rolled down my face.

"I miss home. Said Mel. "I think I have a stomach ache. You say 'It could be worse', but I don't see how." She cried quietly. I put my arm around her and looked back at Mom.

"Our Father who art in heaven, hallowed be Thy Name." Mother began.

During the prayers Melanie held her sides.

"Dad! I see some yellow lights at the bottom of this mountain. That must be the Castle! Look!" I cried out.

"Thank God, Billy. At least we're getting close to something. Oh, Lord, please if you would...let this be it?" Mother implored. She held her knuckles to her face.

In a minute, the Castle appeared in view a half block away. Four grey cobblestone columns surrounded the driveway. Cream-colored canvas drapes flanked the entrance. The approach was a visual feast. The gigantic doors were crafted in elaborate, yellow stained glass and black wrought iron. Massive Spanish style gas lamps positioned on either side of the doors created intense romantic ambience and authentic medieval grandeur.

"I can hardly believe my eyes!" She dabbed her eyes with a handkerchief. "Thank you for finding it. I know it wasn't easy driving down that mountain!"

"Thank the Lord. I was beginning to wonder." He pulled the car to a stop, and they looked at each other relieved. He reached over for her hand, squeezed it, looked her in the eye, and then got out of the car abruptly. "I'll be back in a minute. Sit tight."

One by one heads popped up in the back seat.

"Are we here?" said Anne rubbing her eyes.

"Is this the Castle?" said Valerie, still groggy.

"Thank goodness! I'm getting hungry again!" said Liz, shaking her frousty head.

"Take a look at this mansion we'll be staying in tonight! It looks like a dream castle—right out of a picture book!" said Mom.

"It reminds me of Sleeping Beauty's castle, Mom." Anne said.

I can't believe we're really staying here overnight!" said Allie. "I hope it's not a mistake!"

Dad returned pale but happy.

"Everybody out! This gentleman will show us to our rooms. Everyone grab something. We don't have to unload the top of the car. We're only staying one night." Dad instructed. We each took a bag and stepped into our castle disbelievingly. Enchanted, we stood gaping at a splendid Great Hall surrounding us.

"Follow me, gang!" He began marching to the stairs at the end of the hall. "Keep your chin up and keep moving forward! C'mon gang. We're late for dinner!" Dad was at the foot of the stairway as the gang eased down the picturesque hall, soaking in artifacts of medieval life which surrounded us. I sensed we were crossing a boundary line into a fantasy world of fables, fairy tales, dungeons, princesses, romance and heroism.

"I've got to stop and drink this in. It's fantastic." I thought about Macbeth and Hamlet. "It's like being in another world!"

"C'mon gang. Move. We'll come back to look at it later. Dinner was served at 8:00 p.m.!" said Dad.

"Hey what about an elevator?" Jimmy asked.

"Jimmy, all afternoon sitting in a car, and you want to ride an elevator up one story? I can't believe my ears!" Dad said.

"This bathing suit bag's heavy, Dad. I think Marie put some books in it."

We climbed the wide spiral staircase. At the sharpest point in the curve, to the right of a tall stained-glass window stood a life size knight's coat of armor. We stopped to stare.

"Hi, there!" Anne addressed the knight. The mouth plate on the armor snapped shut.

"He's mean, you all." She said, trailing behind us.

Soon as we got in the room Mother stuck her head in.

"Freshen up, everyone, and we'll go down to dinner. But please don't drink the water!"

Jimmy began jumping on the beds. Anne followed. Soon it was everyone.

"A castle! I can't believe it. A castle to spend the night in!" said Jimmy.

"There's something so real about it, it's almost spooky." I said.

"Spooky? I was scared to death coming down that hall. It's like a different world and you don't know what could happen next!" said Mel.

"It looks like the place they film the Zorro shows. Look out of this window, Marie." Valerie pointed out. "Can't you see Zorro popping around out on that wrought iron balcony?"

The window overlooked a courtyard with gardens and a lighted fountain in the center. Most appealing, but it was the quiet around the place that made it feel haunted. It seemed like a movie set, a spy intrigue maybe, and we were inadvertent main characters walking in something over our heads.

We filed into the Castle's dining room just as the maitre d' was getting ready to close up. Standing at attention, we were hopeful, eager, starving, in love with the place.

"There's no one in here." Jimmy noticed. "Maybe the food's bad."

"Jimmy, stop. It's past their usual closing time." I said.

"I know it's a little late, but my children are starved. Can you take care of us?" Dad was cordial, amiable and diplomatic; it may have been impossible for anyone to turn him down.

We took places around a large table, relieved and hopeful.

"This doesn't look bad! It's magnificent in here!" I was bowled over. "It's everything we pictured, Dad!"

"And the food is supposed to be excellent, too!" he said opening the menu. "Butsie, I'm ordering the nicest steak they make. A Chateaubriand! That's what they do best down here." Dad said.

"I had steak for lunch today though." She said.

"It doesn't matter! We need a little extra strength for the journey. I think we'll order steak for everyone, for that matter!"

While waiting for the Maitre D' to return, Dad closed the menu, folded his arms on the table in front of him and smiled.

"Do you kids know you've got the greatest Mom in the world?" he asked looking around for answers.

"I agree." I said.

"Your mother is a real pioneer woman, girls. I can tell you, she's not the type to crumble easily! She's no porcelain teacup. Your mother has lots of courage and character, and sometimes I don't know where I'd be without her!" he said practically choking with pride.

"Stop that. I appreciate the compliments, but let's call the waiter. They're a little put out with us for coming here so late."

Dad got up and returned with the waiter. He ordered Chateaubriand and Caesar salad for everyone. The waiter nodded his assent as if someone had socked him in the stomach. He left and we assessed his reaction. "It's not right to come in here so late and order a full course meal. They want to go home. What can you do?" said Mom.

"I wonder how many families with seven children come in here to eat. And look at the way we're dressed! Maybe we should be getting a hamburger!" I said.

"Right, but we didn't see McDonalds anywhere." Said Dad.

"Life isn't worth living if you can't be yourself. Be happy with yourself don't worry what others think of you."

Dad smiled and began singing softly.

The girl that I marry will have to be

As soft and as sweet as a symphony...

"Don't sing at the table." Said Mom.

...The girl I call my own...

She'll wear satin and laces and smell of cologne...

This is going a bit too far!" Mom became a little flustered.

"Didn't you say there's no point in worrying what people think of you? I want to tell you how much I love you. Who cares what the waiter thinks?" said Dad.

"Alright but enough is enough. Anyway, we tell the children not to sing at the table." Mom fussed.

"Practice what you preach, Dad." Jimmy whispered to Anne.

"What was that, son?" Dad looked over at him.

"Sorry, Dad."

In the room each one found a bed partner. There were two rollaway beds in addition to two twin beds. Anne climbed in beside me.

"It's a pretty place, but it seems strange the way in Mexico you're either in the middle of nowhere, or you're in the lap of luxury. There doesn't seem to be an in-between." Mel observed.

"You've got a point. It has to do with the social stratification system here. They have a small wealthy elite class of landowners, and then a mass of impoverished people who work for them. It's really sad. If I think about it too much, I get depressed." I said.

"Marie thinks she knows everything." Said Jimmy. "All those big words."

"Well, if you want to know what anything means, I'll be happy to explain it to you." I replied.

"It's spooky in this Castle. I didn't see any other customers around the place, did you?" Asked Val.

"No." Said Althea.

"I have a creepy feeling something weird is going to happen here. Do you think this place is haunted?" Valerie went on. A hush fell over the room.

"That closet near my bed gives me the shivers. I can imagine opening it and a skeleton plopping down on me." I said.

"Let's say the Rosary, y'all." Melanie suggested. "Maybe that'll help us get to sleep."

Like a lioness guarding her lair, I remained watchful. There was a lot to absorb. What would the morning bring? Would there be good adventures or a fresh take on the way of the Cross? The little children barefoot in the street had grabbed my heart. Paradoxes kept my mind open.

Images paraded through my mind and I wrote some of them down in a notebook. I wanted to remember the smallest impressions like the men in skimpy ribbed t-shirts revealing ample muscles in the street, the charming caballeros who sang to us in Monterrey, the sniffy, stuffy waiters in the hacienda, an uncooperative bellboy, Allie's pallid face dropped on Mother's shoulder, the words to "America the Beautiful" sung with tears, the chateaubriand consumed in camp clothes, Mother's embarrassment being serenaded in the dining room, the knight's armor clanking shut when Anne spoke to him, the closet to my right near the bed.... what might it contain? The culture around me was an unpredictable place.

Morning arrived cool and dewy. Excitement filled me. Huddling around the Ford wagon waiting for a tour guide, I was happy we wouldn't be lost in this town. A local tour guide might cut down on harrowing misadventures and show us the things we needed to see. I began to suspect that hilarious memories of woeful mishaps might be the biggest takeaway from our travels. Security and good sense would not be ruling the situation.

"Don't need 'em today. No thanks." Dad motioned as he declined the colorful striped blankets from a merchant strolling around the parking area waving them open in front of his nose.

"They might make a bed in the backseat." Mom said, winking at the guy. He kept opening one after the other as Dad looked the other way.

"We could spread out one or two in the back. Even an adult could lie down and take a nap. I like the aqua and pink." I said.

"All set. Where did you put the pesos?" Mom approached Dad.

"The wagon isn't going to hold a truck full of souvenirs, Butz. I hope they can use them." Dad pulled out a wad of pesos. I like the idea of the makeshift bed."

"Buenos dias, Senor. Buenos dias, Senora." Our guide showed up just as the sale was finalized.

"Good morning, good morning, Buenos dias. Senor Pedro?" Dad smiled at him.

"Si Senor."

"Let's have it gang, everyone say good morning in Spanish. 'Buenos dias!"

"Buenos dias!" We yelled out.

"Buenos, dias, Senor Pedro." I rolled my R to get practice. Senor began a conversation with Dad in Spanish. He wanted to drive our car.

"No, no, Senor." Cordial efforts to explain were not going to work and an argument appeared to be possible. "I am always the one to drive this car. All these children.... And insurance..." he pointed. Facial reactions didn't help, gestures did no good and some Spanish and English and Spanglish went back and forth until Pedro climbed in and took the wheel.

Pedro began going on in Spanish using eye expressions and waving his arms up and down, while taking off down the road to the town of Guanajuato. Some words popped out of his mouth which I picked out. Down the road a few blocks, Pedro pulled to a stop to smile wide at a couple of guys selling guayaberra shirts. They were waving their things like the blanket vendors, confident and all-smiles. With Pedro as a friend, why not?

"You have to get one, Billy. It's diplomacy. You can wear it at dinner tonight." She pinched his cheek.

"It might get the wagon started up again, too." I said. "Pedro will wait."

"How much is this tour going to cost me with him driving?" Dad asked, handing over the pesos and smiling at the guy who handed him the yellow shirt.

"Don't sweat the small stuff. Remember that one, Dad?" Jimmy said.

"Now when you take the shirt off your back for your fellow man, you'll have an extra." Melanie chided him.

"Let's get a couple of shirts for Billy and Randy, too." Mom suggested.

"We'll have time to shop for two weeks. Come on." Dad protested.

"This way you don't even have to get out of the car." She answered, looking at the faces of the salesmen.

As they went back and forth, the guys had time to run back to their truck and bring back blankets and paraphernalia. They began shaking out rugs.

"Hey fellows. Watch the way you shake those things!" Mom said, brushing off her blouse. "Let's move along, Pedro." She smiled and Pedro cranked it up.

"May be none of my business, but since when do we leave the driving to a stranger, Dad? Aren't you uncomfortable in the middle seat?" I asked.

"Please drop the subject. We've been through it once. Let's just deal with it." Uncharacteristically, Dad rolled his eyes toward heaven. Senor accelerated and hilarity bubbled up. Mother looked out of the window smiling, dabbing at her lipstick.

This precious village, tiny and quiet, tucked in the mountains, was a gem like the rings Mother imagined. Weaving in and out of narrow cobblestone streets, you could window-shop without stepping out of your vehicle. Each storefront had its own charm and a phantasmagoric variety of offerings. I thought it might be a good idea to stop here and make this the vacation. Just stay at the Castle a few days and head home.

Guanajuato didn't appear to be expecting too many guests. The shopkeepers popped their heads out of the door to look into our world, some to attempt conversation. Pedro made a point of visiting with a couple of friends. The town was built primarily with grey stones and the buildings were attached one to one another along hilly pathways paved and unpaved. Children scurried in and out and Pedro screeched to a stop once or twice to avoid accidents. He yelled at them and kept going on jabbering. Suddenly, he broke into a rehearsed tour in broken English. He gave us the history of the 16th century in Mexico as he made sharp turns, zig-zagging in and out and stopping and starting.

The pedestrians stopped to allow us to pass and peeked in on us as if we were a UFO.

"Hey Pedro, how about showing us a shop with rings?" Mom asked. I wondered if she could have read my thoughts. Don't go further if you can find it here.

"No comprendo, Senora." I concluded that Pedro's friends weren't in jewelry.

Stopping at one of the few red lights in town, a caballero with a huge hat looked into Mother's window, leaning too close for comfort. "Por las ninas, Senora." He showed his teeth with a wide grin and looked back at the car filled with girls. As he shook little bodices and skirts in front of her, she stammered.

"Er, uh...: She wanted to be sweet. It was a question of numbers and time too.

"No gracias, Senor." Dad happily rescued her, signaling adios.

"Adios, amigo." I shouted back to him, catching another view of those bright white teeth and the smile.

"You can't help but love them. And you know what? The way we act determines how they think about Americans, and we want to make friends don't we? You can't change the whole world, but you can start with one person." Mom said, looking at me.

"They keep smiling at us. I guess it's to make a living. But they do make you feel welcome, don't you think? They seem happy we're here. The expressions on their faces are a riot." I said.

"Let's save a few dollars for Mexico and those rings, girls. There are a few towns further south famous for silver things too." All of a sudden Mother's back stiffened up and the whites of her eyes brightened.

"Butsie! What is it?"

She continued to look straight ahead, then nodded slowly indicating he ought to look at what was coming next.

He looked and his jaw dropped. Leaning forward I noticed the cause for alarm – the cobblestone street in front of our vehicle was headed straight down a steep hill. One by one the troopers gasped. Anne screeched. A taxicab arrived on the tail of our wagon, with a driver holding down on an obnoxious horn.

"This car is too wide for our streets, Senor." Said Pedro.

"Maybe we should've taken another route." Dad said, peeved.

"I've got vertigo." I announced. "Get me near the window, quick."

"She likes to show off big words. She's faking." Said Jim.

"This is bad. We may be stuck here!" Melanie suggested. The taxicab driver honked again and again. The driver climbed out from behind his wheel.

"Oh no. I see a bullfight coming." Liz stated.

"Everyone calm down immediately." Mom ordered.

"Look what's coming." Allie said, ducking.

"I said calm down this minute." Mom sounded like there was a prune seed stuck in her throat. "Everyone."

A small Toyota entered the street at the bottom of the hill, and slowly approached us.

"Better get moving." Said Pedro. "This Toyota will have to back out."

There ended the panic, and there began the hysterical laughing.

"This ought to be a one-way street" Cried Liz.

"What next?" Val cackled.

"Things are crazy in Mexico." Said Jim, calling over the girls.

"It's different, that's for sure." Said Mel.

Pedro inched downward. Mother kept peeking in the store windows smiling. "Mexican shopping is easier, I admit. You don't have to step out of your car or park!" Mom chuckled.

Soon we were face to face with the Toyota, war about to break out between the two drivers. Pedro shot him a glare confidently then rested on his horn. When the guy didn't move, Pedro opened up the car door and squeezed out to begin yelling at him words we may need to learn before long.

"Oh no." Mother winced.

"Oh, yes." Val grinned.

"Mexico!" Said Jim. "Where's that word notebook?"

The driver of the Toyota climbed back in disgust, threw his right arm over the front seat to look back down the hill, then put his vehicle in reverse.

"We won the war! Yay, Pedro." Called Liz.

"For he's a jolly good fellow. Bravo. Bravo!" Mel called out.

"We could really learn some Spanish in his car!" Allie said, winking at Jimmy.

"The guy looked mad, and I mean mad." Said Anne. "Hey, his face seems to be getting redder and he's stopping again."

"Shut up you all. He can hear us." I said. Mother swiveled around irked. "Be quiet, I mean."

At the bottom we took a right turn, breathing better. Some cheering broke out.

"When I say three, everyone yell 'adios, amigo' One, two, three – 'adios, amigo!'" Dad said. The chorus was in full volume.

CHAPTER SEVEN

"O.K. Gang. Let me hear you loud and clear! Is everybody happy?"

"Well, yes." The response came back strong enough to pass muster.

"Good going. Let's have a round of "Do-re-mi.' You've got a lot to give! So let's hear it!" He called out.

"Dad," I timidly approached him as the white Ford sped down the two-lane blacktop headed for Mexico City. "Last Spring a film critic came to school and she said that most of what the American public gobbles up at the box offices is purely schmaltzy."

"What?" He asked.

"Schmaltzy. That's how she describes insipid entertainment with absolutely no literary value." I explained.

"What examples did she give of such 'schmaltzy' entertainment?" He inquired.

"She said 'The Sound of Music' was a perfect example." I held my breath.

"Who is this crazy woman? 'The Sound of Music' is one of the best films in history. About a family singing and laughing together!" He balked at the baloney. "Is this gal a communist?"

“Her name is Mother Hargrove. She said people want to escape from reality in over-sentimental fairy-tales.

“A nun said that? Butz, have you heard anything about this woman? I’ll call Reverend Mother Stanley when I get back. What movies does Mother Hargrove think the American people ought to look at, Marie?”

“She showed a movie by the Italian producer Fellini. It was nutty. She analyzed it and called it art.”

“What are you reading lately anyway? That’s better to talk about.”

“You’re right.” I said. It was a relief to know my Dad and I thought the exact same thing about Hargrove.

“*The Fountainhead* – it’s about an architect. He’s a visionary who breaks all the rules and won’t give people what they want in order to make money. The guy wants to make important contributions and build with new concepts. People hate him at first but eventually he gets popular, and becomes an idol. It’s about hypocrisy and ideals.

Ayn Rand was writing about Frank Lloyd Wright.” I said.

“What’s that author’s name?” Dad asked.

“Ayn Rand.”

“I see. What did the book teach you?” He asked.

"It reminds me of Mom when she says don't worry about what people think of you. To do what your heart leads you to do." I said.

"Well said." I learned that lesson a long time ago and I have to practice it often. There are people who hate me for what I stand for, but I can always hold my head up high, because I know I'm following my conscience." He said.

"They hate you because you took a stand on integration?" I asked.

"That and a lot of other things I'm trying to do to help people. In my work as President of the National Housing Conference, we have a goal to provide a decent home for every U.S. citizen! It's not popular with everyone. I believe in helping those who can't help themselves." He explained.

"Let's stop solving the world's problems and say the Rosary." Mother respectfully interrupted.

"I get hate letters regularly, and I laugh at them. It's a compliment! It means I'm doing my job. You have to stir people up and challenge their thinking before any social change takes place!" Dad began to sound victorious.

"I believe in God..." Mother began.

"Sure do hate to bring it up, but I have to go to the bathroom." I anticipated the answer. Dad pretended to be stumped. He eyed the plains to the right and to the left as though he hadn't heard me. He waited for me to repeat the bad news. "I hate to say it, but I have to go."

"Did you know that Queen Elizabeth had to wait eight hours to go to the bathroom when Parliament was in session?" He replied.

"You've told me that in family meetings. It doesn't help the problem. I still have to go, and I'm not Queen Elizabeth."

"You don't have a problem. It's a challenge! Think about something else for a while until I see a gas station, tomato." I pictured an embarrassing mess, if he wanted to be stubborn. The Queen Elizabeth speech never helped.

"Laugh at yourself, sweetie. We'll get there." Mom offered.

"I'm afraid laughing would not be the thing at the moment, Mother. Thank you, though." I answered.

"We can sing 'a hundred bottles of beer on the wall'. That makes time pass fast!"

"Not good y'all."

"What about 'Take Me Out To The Ball Game'?" Dad said.

"Great!" Came the squad.

Take me out to the ball game,

Take me out to the crowd.

Buy me some peanuts and crackerjacks,

I don't care if I never get back;

Cause it's root, root, root for the home team

If they don't win it's a shame,

Cause it's one-two-three strikes you're out,

At the old ball game. What a game!

"That's right up your alley, Liz! I never can get over how you make such good grades even though you're always so busy with basketball and volleyball!" I said.

"It's no problem." She said airily.

"Let's have a round of 'School days'!" Dad smiled wide as he led "School Days. If gush could be measured on a graph, he went over the chart. Then "Eastside Westside" and "You're A Grand Old Flag". The sequence came from the blue spiral bound family songbook Dad had created. Daddy squeezed Mother's hand as he came to "The Bicycle Built for Two" and choked on the lines. A tear appeared in Mother's eye and she dabbed it quickly with a perfumed handkerchief she kept in her purse. She fanned herself with an ivory fan from the Castle gift shop.

"Keep your eyes on the road, Billy." She put his hand back on the steering wheel.

"Oh, Butz, what's the matter?"

"God is good to us, Billy." With her eyes still moist, she began to laugh sounding as though halfway between tears and humor. She looked back at us and pronounced her golden rule for living well: “You can’t take it with you.”

“When Irish Eyes are smiling....” Dad began his favorite Irish tune filled with pride. He sounded like there was an egg stuck in his neck.

“No way, Billy. Enough is enough. Please! Not that Irish malarkey.” Mom sobered up quickly, waving her hand.

“Malarkey? What do you mean malarkey! Excuse me. I love my Irish heritage. Aunt Gerdy and my father were half-Irish. They taught me all those songs!” I agreed with Mother.

“Let’s not get started on all your relatives and ancestors, please. That’s almost as bad as when you and Marie start in on the world’s problems. It’s like a broken record!”

“I love to talk about my relatives and ancestors. How will anyone know about them? The kids I mean. It’s history.”

“I’m sure of that! It’s history alright.” Jimmy said.

“Dad’s ancestors taught him all the things he wants to teach us!” Mel said.

“Right. We take our character and ideals from those who have gone before us. That is, if we want to learn the lessons of life from them.” He said.

“Hey, how many more miles until we get there, Dad?” Liz asked.

A little daydream came up. We had gone for one of Father Romagosa's afternoon Masses and Mom stopped to invite him to Sunday brunch which she didn't need to do, because he always showed up anyway. In the dream, Mom drove home via Simon Bolivar Avenue and pulled to a stop in front of the Leidenheimer Baking Company, founded by her great grandfather George Leidenheimer in 1896. She sent me in to pick up two 4-foot long brown bags filled with French bread loaves which had come out of the oven bent. They couldn't fit into the usual paper sleeves so we got them really cheap. I broke off the Pope's nose, the very end of the loaf which looked like a long, narrow nose and snitched a delicacy. At home, between chores with dinner prep, I buttered up a huge pan of French bread cut in inch-thick slices. We used the toasted rounds to soak up sauces from the meat. Mom insisted we refer to gravy as "sauce." Tasted like gravy to me. The dream moved on to lunch at school the next day where I opened up my sandwich to find no filling. Did my sister put me on a bread-only diet? Thanks a lot! My friend Caroline asked me why I always had French bread sandwiches. I told her I liked it that way, what was her problem? Inside I wondered why we had to use those rejected bent loaves. Next, it was Sunday dinner. I bit into my French bread and Father Romagosa smiled from across the table, then remarked: "Once past the lips, forever on the hips." I seethed. The nerve, as rotund as he was!

"How many more miles, Dad!? I'm getting sick of this driving in Mexico. I'm ready to get there!" said Jimmy.

"Jimmy, don't let me hear any of that complaining. I want to make men out of you. Men don't complain and gripe. Find the map, girls."

The scramble for the map began once again. "I can't understand why you people can't keep the map in one place and leave it there." Dad's vexation motivated quick action.

"It would seem reasonable but everyone keeps changing their places like musical chairs. And we have a few different map readers. It gets moved around a lot." Melanie explained.

"Jimmy, you're squishing my leg. Get off!" said Anne indignantly.

"I'm just looking for the map, kid. Don't you care, little girl?" said Jim.

"Bully!" Anne cried.

"Pest!" Jimmy shot back.

"Grouch!" Anne returned insult for insult.

"Ahem." Mother cleared her throat. "Let's say a prayer to St. Anthony, he'll find the map." After the Hail Mary, Althea squealed victoriously and dragged the map out from between seat cushions.

"I found it! St. Anthony sure is great, isn't he?" said Althea like she was discovering a new toy.

"It seems superstitious to me." Said Mel. "Like that woman who told you that you had a money mole, Mom." Melanie said. "You believe all that?"

"Well isn't praying to St. Anthony about the same thing as believing in that voodoo?" Melanie continued.

"Think whatever you want, darling, that's up to you. I only know how I find things when I need them." Mom replied judiciously.

"Where are we?" I asked.

"Take a look at the map and tell me what you see, Marie Louise." Dad came out of his own think-tank.

"Give me a minute. I'm finding it. Let's see." I responded.

"God, I feel so jammed in back here! Push over, Melanie!" Came Val.

"Over? Valerie, you're crazy. Marie, you heard Dad—read that map!"

"I'm getting sick of Mexico." Added Jim.

"I'm getting sick in Mexico. I have a stomach ache." Said Anne.

"Try to be pleasant, children. It won't be much longer." Mom pulled a comb out of her purse and touched up her hair, then passed the comb back to Melanie. “Everyone take a turn and comb your hair. We should be getting out soon.” Tactics like these were supposed to instill hope in the restless. It was something to do. Next it was to clear the gum wrappers and other stuff.

“Like bull!” Mumbled Jimmy.

“What did I hear you say back there, son?” Dad asked.

“Nothing.” Jim replied.

“I see. Keep a good disposition. Once in a while we need to practice patience. Remember Queen Elizabeth and it won’t seem so bad.”

“Once we get into Mexico City we’ll be in a beautiful hotel, as nice as the Castle. We’ll stay there for three days, spread out and get comfortable.” Dad announced.

“Come on, Marie. What says the navigator?”

“I’m giving the map over to Mom. Maybe you can find where we are, Mother.” I gave up and gave over the map, defeated.

“When are we getting past, Mexico, I still want to know?” came Anne. Laughter and giggles broke out in the back.

“You’ll never get anywhere with negative thinking, gang! You have to think positive every step of the way! Then you’ve got the world by the tail!” Dad crowed.

"Great!" Came Liz, tongue-in-cheek. "I just want to get there!"

"We better stop the car and concentrate on finding out where we are." Dad finally resigned himself to figuring out our whereabouts. He pulled to a stop on the side of the road. Everyone near a door opened it.

"You idiot! Get off!" Mel fussed.

"Melanie!" Mother eyeballed her with consternation.

"Mom, Valerie crawled right over my legs and now I'm aching. It's not fair!" Mel fretted.

"I have to get some air. I've got claustrophobia." She began to do jumping jacks on the grass.

"Dad, I'm going to go to the bathroom here." I said.

"No you're not. You can forget that. There's not even a bush. You'll have to wait, dear." Mom popped.

"I can't wait. Mom. Please. I have to go."

"Well..." alright, Marie, get out of the car. Everyone turn your head and look at the highway, so she can go to the bathroom." Mother sucked in air working hard to put up with this.

"Marie Louise is going to the bathroom on the highway!" Jimmy cheered.

"No, she is going to the grass!" Valerie corrected, laughing loudly.

"You're next." Mother said to her.

"This is really getting fun. I wish Billy and Randy were here for this. Would they ever get a kick out of this! It's great! I can't wait to tell them about it." Added Jim, roaring.

I did the best I could to ignore them all, relieved myself, and got back in the car. "When are we getting there, Dad?"

"Looks like we'll be there in about one short hour, kids. How about that? Just one hour to go and we're in Mexico City!" He seemed to be expecting a cheer.

"An hour? My God I can't take it!" Valerie complained shocked at the bad news.

"That will be a 50 word composition, child." Mom noted.

"50 words! Mom! I'm not Marie!"

"50 words!" She said emphatically.

Dad started up the car.

"Come on kids, cheer up. Things could be worse. Think positive. Let's have a song. How about a round of "As the Caissons Go Rolling Along?" Come on! Let's hear it loud and strong!" He started it up "Over hill over dale, as we hit the dusty trail..." Come on kids I can't hear you!"

"Okay dad. Come on you all, let's sing! One. Two. Three. 'Over hill over dale, as we hit the dusty trail..."

"Dusty Trail." Jim chuckled. I see why you picked that one Dad. All you can see out there is one big bunch of dust!"

"...as the Caissons go rolling along!" the gang finished with a bang.

"You know kids, your Mother and I really wanted each and every one of you to come along. We prayed that God would send us a child, and each time He answered our prayer." He expounded, revealing more personal thoughts.

"Dad, what makes you think we don't feel that you wanted us?" I asked.

"I just want you to know how much we wanted each of you, and how much we love you."

"Well, thanks, Dad." I replied. "But, Mom. Was it hard having so many children right in a row?"

"Not really. Nothing's hard if it's what you want and you feel it's what God wants for you. And besides, having a child is the healthiest thing in the world for a woman!" She beamed and looked at Dad.

"Your Mother is a real pioneer woman, kids!" Dad bragged.

"Cut that out, Billy. I'm no pioneer. I'm just Butz."

"Butsie. My Irish Rose. The Girl that I Married." He blew her a kiss.

"Keep your eyes on the road, Billy."

"I'm thirsty." Said Anne.

"The pioneers had to go for miles and miles in covered wagons before getting water." Dad told her.

"What does that have to do with it?" She griped.

"Remember that tableau we saw last year at Knott's Berry Farm about life in the covered wagons?" I reminisced. "It gave me the creeps. It made me feel horrible. I could have never stood it! I felt so sorry for those poor children going all that distance in a rickety wagon. It made me realize how spoiled we are!"

"Well, I don't want any of you to be spoiled, children. I'm raising you to be pioneers. I want to make men out of you!" Said Dad emphatically.

"Not that again." Came Mom. "Billy, I asked you to stop that!"

"I want these kids to have character and perseverance. I want them to be leaders, and not to wilt when the going gets rough!" He explained.

My thoughts turned back to the conversation about how they really wanted all of us. "I know at least one of us that Mother really wanted!"

"Who's that, Marie?" asked Dad.

"It's Jimmy." Everyone in the back gasped. "Yes, Jimmy! When I was eight years old, I went to Dr. Freddie Vaughn's office with Mom. I didn't know for sure why we were going to Dr. Vaughn's when Mom wasn't pregnant, but I guessed. Mother never answers too many questions. We got there, and she left me in the waiting room to read Highlights on the green leather sofas. When she came out she announced to me that she was having another baby. She acted like she was the Queen for a Day. When we were leaving the office, Mother and I began to plan an announcement party!"

Jimmy looked puzzled. Then he shrugged and smiled contentedly.

CHAPTER EIGHT

The asphalt jungle of Mexico City stretched out in every direction in front of us, and the urban kid inside me felt more at home. Six million people! Whew!

Sailing into sprawling infrastructure, Dad became anxious. “Hey people heads up! Where’s the map? This isn’t a good place for a wrong turn.” A mad scramble, then Mom opened the map thanking St. Anthony.

“I think you already took the wrong turn Billy. Don’t worry. We’ve made it here and no one’s starving yet. We’ll get there.” She said. “Let’s thank God.”

“St. Anthony, too.” Liz suggested.

“Make an offering. He likes money for the poor.” She said.

“Saints aren’t supposed to be interested in money.” Melanie frowned.

“If it’s to feed the poor, they are.” Mom explained.

Frousty heads began to pop up after naptime on the colored quilts. The myriad sights, sounds and aromas of the City caused a hush of wonder to settle over the travelers. People were perched with necks craned. Billboards in Spanish piqued curiosity and colorful Latin images seemed appealing. I scribbled down words and would later look them up in my Spanish English Pocket Dictionary.

"It's just one wrong turn. There couldn't be too many arteries leading to the center of town. The guidebook says the hotel is right smack dab in the middle of the city. Look for the next chance to get back on the interstate we got off of. That's the one that will take us right to the central square of town." Mother calmly explained.

"I can't stand wasting all this time." Dad pulled over and grabbed the map. Mom conferred with him studiously and they both concluded she had the right idea.

"Why don't you let me drive, Billy. You can navigate. You must be exhausted after driving so far." Dad yielded the wheel and braced himself with the map as she took off smiling. Backseat travelers began warming up.

"6,000,000 people in one city. Gosh! That's one huge city wouldn't you say?" came Val.

"It's hard to imagine when you think about it." I said ponderously.

"Hey, what's the population of New York City, anyhow?" asked Melanie. "Isn't it about the same?"

"Ask Marie Louise. She ought to know that." Jimmy piped up.

"The population of New York City is roughly 7,000,000." I replied.

Minutes later, we were gliding along a lush tree-lined boulevard and marveling at the inviting square park to our left landscaped with flowering botanicals and adorned with Grecian style statues. A postcard- perfect scene.

"Looks like this is the center of the town. It's dreamy!" Mom said. To the right, I noticed a semicircular set of Corinthian columns surrounding a fountain and a Greek style statue of a young man taking the air in his birthday suit.

"Look to the right! It's a hotel that looks like a palace." Heads turned in unison and there were a few gasps. We beheld a palace—a white columned high-rise hotel which stretched the block long.

"It's magnificent! Wonder what goes on in there." Mom asked.

"Believe it or not, I think you're looking at the Alameda Hotel. On the map it looks as if it's right across from the central square!" Dad announced, amazing even himself.

"You've got to be kidding me. That's the Alameda? Oh, Lord! Oh no, children!" Mom yelped in a panic. She turned her head around afraid to look at the condition of her group. "Everyone please comb your hair immediately! Marie, pass your comb around—we don't have time to lose. Do you think with all our gang it will be appropriate? We aren't prepared for this one!"

She said as she gazed at the palatial white structure.

"Don't worry about a thing, Butz. Just do me a favor and swing into the driveway on your right." He said.

"Anything you say, darling." Mother pulled to a stop and went to work with the comb. "If there's anything I hate, it's showing up like a bunch of hillbillies."

"Hillbillies! Mother said we look like a bunch of hillbillies! Hahaha—we'll be like the Beverly Hillbillies! The new image was unanimously accepted and embraced. It seemed like a laugh riot with possibilities and it stuck.

Mother breathed deep gathering dignity. Dad stepped out of the car hoping to locate a bell captain. A man in uniform arrived promptly. He was tall, stately and wore a grey and maroon double-breasted suit and black top hat. His stiff manners reflected training to serve the elite clientele of the Alameda. His eye browsed over our crowded vehicle, studied the bulging 3-foot canvas piled on top, and finally rested on the lady in charge herself. He acknowledged her respectfully with a nod of the head and a kind smile. He returned to a businesslike posture to speak to Dad.

"Hello. I mean buenos dias, amigo!" Dad burst forth buoyantly.

"Buenos dias, Senor." Came his sober reply.

"How about giving me a hand unpacking this car? This is the Alameda, isn't it?" Dad requested with a jovial attitude.

"Yes, Senor. This is the Alameda." He replied politely. "Are you sure you want to stay in the Alameda?" He looked over at the carful once again, returned his eye to Dad and gravely suggested that the price might be very high.

"I'll go into the Registration Desk and check this matter out, sir. Thank you." Dad charged into the hotel with aplomb and importance – confident in his plaid short sleeve shirt.

"Oh children, what could be more embarrassing? The bell captain doesn't think we can afford to stay here!" Mom fussed. A wave of laughter surged up through the car.

"Take it with a grain of salt, Mom!" said Liz. "Isn't that what you always tell us?"

"You always say—'Water off a duck's back'. Don't let it get you. It's funny, Mom!" I said. The idea to come to Mexico was starting to feel like a winner.

"Mom, I told you we didn't have enough clothes." I reminded her. Mom broke into a chuckle and held her handkerchief to her nose as if she had a cold. "This is too funny. When you come to think of it – it's all too funny."

Dad returned to undo the load on top of the wagon and the bell captain lightened up a bit. Campers and the ladies in the middle seat climbed out and straightened up. When the cart was piled high with a load of totes and suitcases, Mother took a playful look at the sight.

"I always said—you can tell a lot about a person from the looks of their luggage." She laughed shaking her head back and forth in disbelief.

Dad wiped his forehead a couple of times as he pulled down larger bags which had been packed underneath everything else. The bell captain stared at him yanking suitcases as if everything about this man was unusual. Dad smiled as he deposited each bag on the cart and then climbed to reach for another.

Mel and I went exploring. The two of us inched our way into the lavish lobby which stretched out like a baseball field. Absorbing the splendor, I wished I could turn invisible. It was so classy, such a romantic place to meet other young people and I felt unprepared. Chandeliers six feet in diameter and groupings of huge carved furniture seemed a like mirage, and sounds of well-dressed Mexican aristocrats quieted other thoughts.

"What are we going to do about these clothes, Mal? I never thought I could feel this way but I'm embarrassed." Mel said. "Can you believe Mom isn't even worried? She's acting like we shouldn't be the least bit bothered about it. Usually, she wouldn't go someplace if she weren't dressed correctly. Remember that visit to the Warwick? She didn't take any of us in there."

"We pretend we don't care about it, either. We keep our chin up, Mel, stick our noses in the air. Let them think we don't know how to act. We're from another country, right?" We laughed and sauntered over to the elevator to read some ads.

"What a kick! Too bad Billy and Randy aren't here. It's the wildest time we ever had! Here comes the elevator. Let's go up to the Lounge on the top floor." Melanie jumped into the plush elevator, smiled mischievously, even flirtatiously, at the operator. She stammered out her "Buenos dias" without a thought that the little flicker in her eyes was quite dangerous. Then she pointed her finger up. "Top floor, sir. The Lounge." He looked at her funny, studying her from head to toe. Melanie could see he hadn't understood her, and pointed to the picture of the Lounge on top of the hotel displayed inside the car. He turned around and pressed the button, then stole a glance at her again. When we stepped out and the doors closed behind us, Melanie laughed out loud. "That guy just kept looking at me like I was crazy. What's so odd about coming up to see the sights up here?"

"I guess a teenage girl dressed in shorts wanting to go to the Bar in the middle of the day looks funny to him." I conjectured.

"Hmm. Now I get it." The cackling began. Some fellows relaxing at the bar straightened up and turned their heads. We quieted down. One of them got up and came over. We headed for the fountain to the right in an escape attempt.

"Oh no, we're being followed!" I said. "Just ignore them. Got it Mel?" The guy backed off. We went over to the balcony, took a deep breath of city air and headed backed to the elevator. For five minutes in the Sky-View Lounge of the Alameda we were suddenly women, not girls.

"Where on earth have you girls been?" queried Dad as we rejoined the hillbillies. "I've been looking all over for you!"

"We wanted to get a look around in the hotel. We rode the elevator up to the Bar!" Popped Mel unabashed.

"The Bar? Great." Said Jim. "Melanie and Mal decide to dash off to the bar the minute they get out of the car. That's cool! Leaving me to unload. Terrific. Nice work, girls."

"Actually, it's ladies. The martinis were excellent." I said.

"Did we get the looks up there, or what?" Mel said.

"I didn't realize Melanie and I were so attractive, Dad. You better keep your eye on her. She's dangerous and doesn't even know it. Either that or the men around here have strange taste in women." I gave the news.

"Dad and Mother looked at each other stumped. This was a new one. "I doubt you two belong in a bar, girls, in the mid-afternoon."

"We just went to take a look..." I said, and Mel looked at Mother like an angel.

The Bell Captain flung open the door to our suite and we stampeded in.

Like a cluster of unstylish country mice huddling and afraid of the unknown, we stopped and stared around us. The living room alone was huge and spacious, sumptuous in decor, and commanded a breathtaking view of the city. It was a penthouse suite.

"This is the President's Suite. He always stays here when he is in Mexico City. In fact, Senor, the President of Mexico just left this suite this morning." First came momentary stupefaction—and then wild fits of hysteria. Jimmy rolled on the floor.

"Can you get over it—we're staying in the President's suite. The President of Mexico was in here this morning! Us- the Beverly Hillbillies—in the President's suite?" Jimmy sounded like he was using a megaphone. The Bell Captain smiled brightly. The phone rang. He answered it.

"No, Senor, El Presidente no es esta ...."

"So it's true. The President of Mexico had just vacated this suite!" Melanie said.

Mother asked if she could get a little fresh air. The bell captain proudly pranced over to the picture window and with no apparent effort shoved it wide open.

"My Lord. Honestly! This window opens up too easily. You can close it right away sir!" She pointed to all the kids. Smiles of comprehension and compassion once again. He departed our company well-amused, and cheerful.

"I've heard it all, Billy. Can you imagine having a picture window that pops right open? That could be extraordinarily dangerous. Children, none of you are to open this window, do you hear me?" Mother ruled, passing around a stern warning.

"Yes, Mother." Valerie said.

"I think I feel faint." Mom said, and sat down on the sofa.

"I guess they weren't expecting a bunch of kids in this suite, honey. It's pretty nice isn't it, Butsie?" He said, sliding his arm around her shoulder, hopeful.

"It's beautiful. We're lucky, Billy. I need a nap though.... soon." She replied.

The telephone rang. "I'll get it." Jim said, marching over to the receiver, straightening his back. He picked up. "No, Senor, El Presidente is taking a walk. He will return in an hour." Clunk.

"How dare you, show off!" Anne went over, pretending to get ready to hit.

"It was easy." Another ring came. "Buenos dias!" He turned to Allie and whispered "I'm learning Spanish. This is fun." Then back to the line. "No, no, El Presidente...."

Dad hired a guide to show us all around the vicinity. Alfredo was his name and in a spirit of joviality, he turned into "Mom's Mexican boyfriend." Didn't he wish! He drooled over Mom admiringly for the next few days while showing us around. He was short, maybe about five-two, and slender, with a square frame. His skin was dark reddish-tan, leathery from smiling. His loving countenance glowed continuously and we had no idea why. The crow's feet and laugh lines drew us to him as to a benevolent camp counselor.

Alfredo stood his ground center stage in the lobby of the Alameda Hotel waiting to meet the Guste gang, ready to welcome us. *Does he know what he is in for? I think he'll regret this.* The man appeared innocent, hopeful—like a lamb to the slaughter. He wore a rumpled navy suit and a tie, tied too tight. He seemed a friendly affable fellow with nothing but goodness in his heart. It wasn't difficult for us to pick him out. He was obvious to me the instant we poured out of the elevator and spotted him, and we headed towards him with no hesitation. The gang swarmed over in his direction like bees to a beehive. With handshakes, naming names, little laughs and flirtatious jokes we became introduced and showed our better side. He behaved as though charmed.

"Alfredo, may I ask you a question about your name?" I ventured. "I thought Alfredo was an Italian name!"

“Aw, come off it, smarty. What do you know about that?” Jim checked my remarks.

“When Memere took Mel, Susan and I to Rome, we ate at a famous restaurant named Alfredo’s. That’s why I thought Alfredo was an Italian name.” I explained.

“Well, you’re wrong. Isn’t she Alfredo?” he laughed. “Stupid.” *Anything to get attention.*

“Perhaps there is an Italian name which is Alfredo, and there is a Mexican name which is Alfredo as well. I only know that I am a Mexican. I promise you that!” A bright smile and straight white teeth gleamed. Dad brought the car around.

“What are we going to see today, Senor?” I asked.

“Today, I am going to drive you all around Mexico City, God willing.” He replied in a matter-of-fact tone. “That means, if God is willing then we will do what we plan on doing.” He explained. It sounded like he was saying “Got Wheeling.”

“I get it. It’ll happen if it’s God’s will.” I clarified for the others mainly.

“Yes. That is exactly what I mean. If Got is wheeling.”

“Speaking of plans, I don’t know if my Dad is going to let anyone else drive his car. You see last time...” I was starting to explain when Dad loped over and joined us.

"Hey gang, I see you've met our tour guide. Hello there, Senor, I mean- buenos dias! Pardon me. I'm Billy Guste from New Orleans! Great to meet you. I see you've been making friends with the children."

The two began planning our itinerary with Alfredo's supernatural third party included in the discussion. As a result, Dad somehow became "wheeling" for Alfredo drive the car and navigate. We were shocked.

"Have you already forgotten that wild ride in Guanajuato? Dad, come on. If that happens in the little town of Guanajuato, what on earth is going to happen here?" I asked.

"This is a huge metropolis, sweetie. It's not going to be easy for Alfredo to tell us anything about the city if he's constantly telling me where to turn. He knows the driving customs down here and where we're headed. I think we ought to just place our trust in him and in God." *You know something's different when Dad allows a stranger to drive his car. And he doesn't usually explain decisions. He must be thinking it through himself. Maybe he's exhausted.* Mother stepped out of the elevator.

"Hey, here's my first lady. Don't you look beautiful, honey!" She strode over beaming, greeted Dad with a kiss and hug and swirled around to say hello to our new best friend. Alfredo fell immediately into a trance over her. He might have expected a feminine blimp after socializing with her multitudinous offspring. He was deferential and adoring to Mother from the moment he met her. She was poetry in motion, a miracle woman—like a goddess from another planet.

"Good morning, Senora." He tipped his head and his heart in her direction.

"Buenos Dias, Senor Alfredo." She smiled at him in a haze of maternal pride and grace, understanding why he was so respectful—accepting the regal position he was giving her. "Isn't it amusing? We're saying Buenos Dias, and Alfredo says 'Good Morning'. Isn't there something a little strange about that?"

"Hey, you all, get it? We're trying to speak Spanish to be nice, and Alfredo's speaking English to make us feel at home! What a riot!" came Jim. "What a hoot!"

"O.K. gang, let's all pile into the car." Dad instructed and then took a few minutes to ease Mother into letting Alfredo drive.

"I have a vivid memory of the shock, coming down that narrow inclined street in Guanajuato. You don't forget things like that easily." She told him. But God was willing, and by and by, Mom was too.

Alfredo assumed the wheel with pride, confidence, hope and cheer—bright eyed and bushy tailed. "Now I am going to show you all around Mexico City." He was in love with his home, his work and the Guste gang, it seemed.

Information and interesting tidbits, legends and historical dates cascaded forth for hours as we threaded our way in and out of the busy, noisy streets of Mexico City. From Alfredo one couldn't help but catch a sense of the sheer loveability of the many sides of Mexican life. He droned on and on. We craned our necks until we were exhausted and grumpy.

"Back to the hotel, God willing!" Finally he announced he was wrapping it up for the day.

"Whew. Thank God that He's willing. I am getting so tired of being in this car, Dad." Said Val.

"Me too. When's dinner?" said Liz.

"And what are we having. What's best in Mexico City?"

Second day in the nation's capital. Mexico City. A different civilization indeed. It was supposed to be the day to go out to the pyramids and tour ancient Aztec ruins, but the Ford developed internal disorders as if in sympathy with her numerous suffering passengers. When it wouldn't start, it seemed like it might be the start of a bad day, and everyone became cranky.

"So what, kids. You can't take it with you!" That slogan consoled Mom, helping her bounce off many a setback. She grinned as if she'd won a prize. It was a golden opportunity to wear her pearls of wisdom.

"Aw, Mom we got dressed to go and we're all in gear. It even sounded interesting. Now what are we going to do all morning?" Liz complained.

"How about a swim?" She said.

"Great! I'm all for that!" came Val. "I wasn't looking forward to crowding into that car again anyway. What were we going to see today anyway?"

"The pyramids but God must not have been willing. You see, I am right about something once in a while!"

"Gee, they even have pyramids in Mexico City?" Liz queried. "I thought they only had those in Egypt."

"We have some pyramids, yes senorita. But they are outside the city, a little drive from here. You see God is good because we did not break down on the way, but before we left."

"Oh." She said.

It was battery trouble and only cost us the morning. Dad got a chance to tune up his Spanish, and the rest of us took a swim and had lunch. We would still make it to the pyramids after all.

On the outskirts of town, Jimmy behaved as if parting with his mother for the first day of nursery school. "I don't think I'm going to like these pyramids, Alfredo." He looked back at the city, and ahead at the dusty plains. "We don't need this part of the tour." Jimmy stated with astounding authority. "It sounds spooky to me, burying dead people with all that stuff of theirs and those people thinking they're going to be living in there. It is weird if you ask me. Sorry,

Alfredo. No offense, but I hate the idea of leaving Mexico City, too. It reminds me of all the time we've spent on the roads in Mexico already. I think I like the Alameda the best of anything we've seen so far."

To our surprise there was enchanting information and folklore to learn on every feature of ancient life. We stayed quiet while Alfredo described their elaborate sewerage system and drainage apparatus. We listened with puzzled delight to his discussion of mosaic art utilized by ancient artisans, and the restoration projects then underway. We heard about various processes used by the Aztecs to make inks and dyes. Alfredo found a spider egg on a lone cactus plant and smashed it on a parking ticket. The color was a beautiful shade of red. We were enthralled. He explained how the Indians would paint stones, ceramic adornments for the home, pits, large vats and the such-like with the paints derived from nature. The legends and technologies expounded upon made it seem almost too fantastic, but still very interesting. He could've told us just about anything.

"This guy knows everything there is to know about all of it. He's a storehouse of info, I'll say that much!" Mom gave me her viewpoint on the way back to wagon.

"There was once a prince and a frog..." Alfredo surprised everyone breaking the momentary silence that passed over the car like an angel on the way back into the city.

"Are we going to have a story this time, Alfredo?" Mom questioned interested. She sometimes enjoyed creative pauses which settled the noisemakers in back. The quiet would come like a dove perched on a fence, but would never stay long.

"I love to tell stories to the children, Senora. It sometimes helps them to take a siesta, for sure. Is that fine with senor and senora?" He asked.

"I love a good yarn. I tell them every night, too. Take it from the top." Dad said.

"And Senora?" He waited.

"Wonderful. Let's hear it!" She was delighted.

"There was once a prince and a frog..." He vacuumed in a couple of listeners who were mesmerized, and promptly put others to sleep.

"Excuse me, Alfredo, did you forget something?" I asked.

"Senorita, you know this one?"

"Can't say for sure. But shouldn't you say, God willing, there was once a prince.... It seems appropriate."

"Senorita is brilliant. A very good listener. I see that I have taught your children some things, Senor." He seemed on the verge of tears of joy.

"Seems like there couldn't be a prince if God weren't willing." At the beginning of his second lecture the other day I had begun counting the "God willings." I gave up on Lecture Number Three. It seemed like every sentence had a "God willing." It was God willing this and God willing that, God willing, God willing, God willing. The expression became infuriating, one minute causing me to snicker and chuckle, another minute making me want to reach over and strangle the guy. God willing, God willing. Am I going to have this refrain going on in my mind in my sleep? It's a slow drip. WHAT IS THIS THING HE KEEPS TALKING ABOUT – GOD'S WILL? If God has a will, what does He do with it? If the cold war heats up and we go to war with Russia or Cuba, does it mean God was willing? Was it God's will, then, for us to have a third world war? If we get in a wreck on the highway in Mexico and get stuck down here, was it God's will, or a mishap caused by inattention? If I get an A was it God's will, or because I studied a lot. If I get an F, was that God's will? Can I blame Him? The entire issue of predestination and God having a will perturbed me because of frustrating paradoxes. He kept it up and each time he'd repeat it, there came a different reaction. There were many mixed messages in our religion and things you couldn't possibly understand. Like the idea that God loves you. They would tell us "God loves you." What could they mean by that, and how do they know anyway. Did God tell Moses by way of a megaphone? So I'm supposed to believe it? How does anyone get that impression, that God loves me individually? Who told them? If God loves anyone, He probably loves me, that's believable, because I'm one of the lucky ones. Have parents who are good to me, love in my home, and have fun friends, but what about the other ones? What about the children down in the Project? Does God love them too, but just forgot about them? Does God love the kids of the migrant workers but allow them to go to bed hungry. Did He just get it all started like the clockmaker God, then let incompetent humans take over? Alfredo's favorite expression was driving me nuts.

Next time it popped out of his mouth, the most surprising feeling came over me—this warm closeness and solidarity with people everywhere.

"There is a great truth, which we believe in our country. Nothing happens without God willing it." Alfredo expounded.

"We believe the same thing, Alfredo. Look at all these kids!" Dad winked and looked into the rear seat to find half the campers asleep.

"Your stories work about as well as the Rosary, Alfredo. I get them to say the Rosary when I want everyone to settle down." Mom told him.

"Oh! Senora, that is so nice." He turned red as he smiled, revealing huge teeth.

The frog turned into a prince, the prince kissed the princess, and those still awake gave Mom her peace and grace, taking a twirl around the Rosary beads. Alfredo recognized the black beads, and nodded, wiping perspiration from his forehead.

Pulling into the circular drive at the Alameda, I jumped out to stretch my legs and arms. Anne climbed out, wrapped her arms around her waist and made a sound like a low growl.

"Anne. What's the matter?" Mom noticed her struggling and ran over to grab her. This kid gets an awful lot of attention the minute something is amiss. It's unfair, but she's the baby. They would tell me to chill out.

"I think we better get to the room. Goodbye Alfredo. And thank you." Mother held Anne close in the elevator. "You see, children, God is good. What if Anne had gotten sick out there on the highway? Aren't we lucky? We're right here at the hotel, and we'll have you there in just a minute, honey!"

Out of the elevator, down the hall the search for the room key threatened to start a war.

"But I just gave it to you a minute ago, Althea. I swear, I just gave it to her, Mom." Stammered Liz.

"I don't allow you children to swear, Elizabeth. Where is the key, Marie?" That hairy eyeball was bad.

"Why am I supposed to know, Mother? It's either Elizabeth or Althea that had it, I promise." *Why am I blamed whenever something like this happens. As if I could solve it faster!*

"Everyone search through your pockets and purses this minute! Anne needs to get into the bathroom right away!" Mother insisted.

"This is ridiculous. We just had that key. Where did it go?" Val was stumped, as everyone frantically foraged through purses dumping contents out on the floor.

Someone giggled. Then someone else. Anne squatted down facing the door, red in the face holding her sides like they would explode.

"There's nothing funny about this situation, girls." Mother replied furious. "I think I could wring someone's neck." She gave us an ominous warning expression, which made Mel break out more. Again came that syndrome—when you shouldn't laugh you want to laugh.

"Get down that hall this minute you two, and find a key to this room! This child is suffering and you think this is some kind of a joke? Truly, I don't know what I am going to do with you two. Go down to the desk THIS MINUTE AND GET THAT KEY!"

"Okay Mom!" We dashed at once.

Sunday wasn't meant to be our day of rest—it was more car repairs for Dad, battery trouble again, a short swim for us, then dressing for Church and the ballet.

Breakfast was light for the majority – toast and Coke becoming the standard. Two toilets were not enough for the activity in the bathrooms; each one had their turn attempting to hurry. There was a line outside the door of people whimpering and banging. How does anyone hurry with loose bowels or worse yet, a bad case of Montezuma's Revenge? This was a chance to learn.

"Hurry in there, I can't wait." Called Liz.

"Queen Elizabeth...." I replied from inside.

"Shut up that garbage and get out of there." She yelled.

"You're waking the dead. Can it." Said Jim from the bed.

Mother entered from the adjoining master bedroom. "What's all this? I just got a call from the management."

Memere had suffered with colitis for years. This was her night of canonization.

There was now a new intention to pray for when Mother said the Rosary – that colitis wouldn't be inherited.

"Okay. Who did it this time? Jim questioned the group while sticking a croissant in his mouth."

"Did what?" I said.

"Who just farted?" Jimmy replied.

Mother's eyes bulged. Her jawbones tightened and flexed, the little blood vessels in her neck protruded out automatically and her posture became rigid. She looked stunned, as if she were about to turn to a stone statue, or explode all over the place—one or the other.

"Mother's not delighted with that talk." I informed him. "Better tone it down." *Perhaps she doesn't feel well either.*

"Who did it? OK. I want to know!" He kept up unafraid of Mom. Mother's head rotated slowly over in his direction; she assumed the rigid manner of a mummy slowly but miraculously returning to life in a late-night horror show.

"I'll not tolerate this form of speech, my child. Do you hear me?" She was angry.

"Yes, Mother. Sorry." He munched on his second croissant and sipped his Coke.

"Oh, Mom, come on. You and Dad are always saying 'what's the use of worrying!' He's just a kid." I tried to calm her.

"It's how you act in your own home that says what kind of person you are. It's not what you do in public that counts the most in God's eyes, but what you do in private. Remember that."

"I know that, but relax. Don't worry about it—he's a kid. He'll learn his manners."

"He certainly will!" Came her indignant, emphatic reply.

Near the water, Mother sat straight to watch the young ones do their dives.

Stricken with Montezuma's revenge, I sat beside her on a chaise lounge. She smoothed some cream on her face with gentle upward strokes, and then tilted her head up to slather it over her neck.

"Mom, the kids always look like they've put in a hard day at camp, but you always look like you just came back from the beauty parlor. How do you do it?" I asked.

"You have to suffer to be beautiful," she said enjoying the sun, looking heavenward.

"What do you mean? You didn't tell me you were suffering. Are you?" She abruptly came to, opening her eyes wide and answered.

"Oh, my gracious, no! Me—suffering? Not on your life! I'm having the time of my life. I must be the luckiest person in the world."

"I never understood this. You tell me you have to suffer to be beautiful when its time to wear high heels, or if I need a girdle. But then you tell me all I have to do is relax and then I'll be beautiful. Somehow it all doesn't add up. It seems like a funny combination. Suffering and relaxation."

"People lose sleep worrying about things. They're only getting old before their time.

Worrying gives you lines on your face. Don't worry about the world's problems. It's okay to think about things, but don't waste time worrying about them. That won't solve a thing."

Now that I had successfully engaged Mother in a one-on-one conversation I jumped at the opportunity to get her to talk to me about her experiences during childbirth. For all she had told me I might still believe the stork brought babies. When I was small, I believed Mom picked a night, went to the Southern Baptist Hospital and chose a baby from a warehouse-size room full of cribs. The real way it happened was never talked about. I was nervous broaching the subject.

"Mom, you had to suffer to have each of us, didn't you?" I came out with it calm and quiet. I knew it was so, but I knew she hid it to protect us.

"Not much, really. Why worry about all those things anyway, honey?" she said.

"You don't have to protect me from the truth. I watch movies and read books, too. I'm a big girl, Mom."

"I've told you this before. It's the most natural and healthy thing in the world for a woman to have a baby. God made it that way. If it was so terrible, how could I have ten of you?" She said.

I came out with it. "Did it hurt, Mom. Come on. You can tell me the truth!"

"They put a gas mask over my face I hardly remember a thing! Now stop worrying!" She turned over and picked up her magazine.

The more she dismissed my concerns, the more convinced I to believe there was a purposefully crafted cover-up designed to protect me from the whole truth. Why does she give me an explanation which she thinks is best for me when I know it is less than the whole truth. She wants to protect me. I am an adult mostly, why can't she understand that? All the closeness she cherishes should include entrusting me with confidences.

Her confidence. Acknowledgement.

I felt isolated in the middle of all this closeness she held so dear.

Mass at the Cathedral of Our Lady of Guadalupe was memorable and enlightening. There were no kneeling benches and the concrete slabs were hard and cold. There were more ladies than men in attendance and hundreds of children. Most of them wore thick black hair tied up and low-cut full-skirted dresses falling down around large hips. The faithful pronounced their prayers loudly with fervent emotion and I could feel the love and faith they were expressing without having to decipher each word. I noticed many chins lifted high as if to point to the Virgin over the Altar, and other chins digging deep into fleshy bosoms. Thousands of candles flickered brightly from small altars lining the sides of the Church.

Passionate love for God was visible all around me. I became swept away in the mood of it, as in a loving trance. The experience of fervor was fleeting, much too short-lived but nonetheless made an indelible impression in my soul.

From the Cathedral, it was on to a reconverted warehouse—a cafeteria- style restaurant in open air. It was surrounded by flea markets and boutiques, some fleas and flies too. Dad asked for the guacamole and tacos, and the rest of us picked our favorite dish. After taking settling with the cashier, Dad had to go in a hurry.

"I'm going with you." Said Jim.

"Me, too." Came Valerie.

"Me three." I said.

Most every one jumped up out of their chair to scurry off behind Dad. He accepted defeat graciously and did a fast walk to the Men's Room. "I didn't think you'd want to come in here, girls! But you insisted on being with me, and since you insisted, come on in!" We laughed and assured him there was no need to be that close. A pharmacy near the men's room beckoned. Mel and I scooted over there playing like it was urgent.

Dad came out of the "Caballeros" bathroom looking wildly funny with frizzed hair and a white moustache of Kaopectate. He marched up to the counter of the drug store.

Before we could get him to wipe off the chalky medicine, he was asking at the counter for more of his new favorite drink. The lady had no clue what he wanted. He repeated the word several times and raised the volume before finally drawing the empty bottle out of his pocket. We didn't tell Mother about it. She might be the next one to get sick.

The Ballet Folklorico was a festive, prismatic kaleidoscope of skirts, legs, oversized colorful umbrellas, and men in sequins. But Montezuma's ghost may have spied his white neighbors in a state of thrill. A surprise attack beset me during the intermission and I was seized by the sharpest pains I had ever felt. I squeezed Mother's arm.

"I have to go back to the hotel. Don't worry. I can walk. I know the way." I told her quietly.

"Absolutely not. I'll go with you." She answered.

"What's this?" Dad overheard. "Marie, what's the matter? You couldn't think of leaving this magnificent spectacle, could you? What's going on?"

"She's sick, darling." Mother interjected.

"I've got to go back, Dad. I love the show but I got an attack. I'm not going to make it."

"I can assure you, you will make it. Now sit right down here beside me!"

He ordered me, then returned to viewing the drama. Mother and I looked at one another. Dad had purchased box seats to get the most out of the internationally famous ballet. I couldn't leave him, especially when I knew he did it for me. I eased down in my chair. Shortly after the curtain rose, the pains tore across my waist and abdomen again. I reached over behind Dad and tapped Mother's shoulder. She knew what to do. We edged out on tip-toes and took baby steps all the way to the hotel, her arm around my waist.

All this for rings but at least we got the rings. Plump, colorful, gleaming rings which had captured Mother's imagination back in Corpus Christi appeared before us bright as expected in a shop down by the Cathedral. The article she had read at the Hilton on Sunday a week ago about these highly touted gem purchases had proved a powerful lure.

It was the second-to-last day in Mexico City. Mother was in rare form, ready for highway robbery she would commit as if in answer to Montezuma and his never-ending revenge. She planned to make the most out of it.

We crossed the giant square early. There weren't too many tourists or locals out yet. It looked like it would be a scorcher, but early the weather was mild and clear, and a blue sky arched over the cobblestone square in the center of town.

"Let's take a picture." Said Dad.

"We don't need one. We have a thousand of those. We need rings." Mom said as if it was perfect common sense, and kept walking.

"We don't have one on this beautiful square. Look at this spot! Have you ever seen a more beautiful sight? Kids, get over there!" He pointed.

"Aw come on Dad, do we have to do this again? It's 9:30 a.m. and we have to take pictures? Please, give us a break!" I chimed in to help Mom.

"Hey, Dad, my shorts are getting dirty anyway by now!" Val said while Dad shoved her into the grouping.

"O.K. everybody 'Smile!' You're not smiling enough! Smile when I say cheese. Okay—cheese! You people must not be awake yet!" He complained.

"They're only children. Can't you give it up this time?" Mom said.

"No. I want everyone smiling. Get back in that shot. 1-2-3 Cheese! All done now where is this place anyway? Where's my map?"

"I think I've got it. Didn't you hand it to me in the car?" She said, digging in her purse. She began studying the map.

Dad whisked it out of her hand immediately. "Let me see that map!" He said excited.

"I was just about to take a look at it." Mom was indignant.

"We're here!" He said, pointing to the center of town. The shop must be over there." He waved his arm to the right.

"C'mon everybody, follow me!" She smiled as she followed her dream.

Inside the shop, the troops were restless. Mom, Melanie and I were enthralled and in love with everything and naturally the shopkeeper was in love with us. Particularly with Mother, figuring that a lady steering her husband into a jewelry store with seven red-blooded children must be possess a powerful sway over the man beside her. He was right.

Dad scooted around in front of the cases in a frenzy making sure to see it all but quick. He craned his neck and scrutinized studiously while his body kept moving forward.

"I tell you what Butsie. I'll take these kids for a walk in the square and see what's nearby while you and the girls shop." He suggested.

"You don't need to leave. Take a look at these rings. The prices are unbeatable!"

"I'm sure of that!" He said.

"I have no idea how I'll choose anything. Everything is magnificent!" she said.

"You'll do a great job of deciding and you'll be better off without me!" He said.

"Without you? Well—if you say so, but...when are you coming back?"

"I'm only going around in the square to look at the other shops through the window. When you're finished, send the girls to get me."

"Well, alright...And thank you." She said smiling."

Dad put his arm around her shoulder. "Now have fun! And take your time...but hurry up!"

Mother, Melanie and I began peering down into the glass cases, and the shopkeeper described the stones and their prices. He showed us indigenous artwork for the neck with corresponding earrings—designs in gold with black onyx. But the colorful plump rings surpassed our dreams—ruby, emerald, topaz, diamond, garnet, aquamarine, rose quartz—you name it. Mother wanted the oval aquamarine surrounded by pearls, and I had my heart set on a rectangular smoky topaz. Melanie went for the opals.

Before Mother sent for Dad he returned, naturally. “Having any luck?” He asked.

“Too much luck.” Mom replied.

Our favorites were approved of by Dad, and the trading began.

“My turn to take a walk,” Mom said. Dad was good at driving a hard bargain.

“If he took fifteen minutes with the vendor selling blankets, we may as well purchase another ballet ticket.” Mother said. “How long do you guess it’ll take?” She asked me.

He was out in no time flat. Apparently he didn’t like it in there much.

“Well did you get them?” queried Mother, in disbelief that he could be finished so fast.

“Yes. Here they are girls! Now come on! Mass is at 11:30.”

“What?” everybody exclaimed in unison.

“Mass is at 11:30 in Our Lady of Guadalupe Cathedral nearby and its going to be over if we don’t step it up!”

“But we didn’t even get a chance to show you the rings.” Said Mom.

“I saw them in the shop. They’re beautiful. Now let’s go! We have to hurry!” He insisted.

"If you say so, Dad." I said.

"Oh, let me catch a quick shot of all of you. No! Marie, take me and Mom and all the rest of us." Said Dad.

"Can't Valerie ever do anything Dad? She's 13 you know." I protested.

"Valerie. Here." He shoved the camera at Valerie's midriff. She bounced off of it and began looking for the button.

Dad grouped everyone together in his long arms stretched out to the right and left, and gave the big cheesy victory grin. "Valerie, say 1-2-3... Cheese. Then snap it."

Butsie and Billy Guste on their honeymoon in Niagara Falls

Yosemite National Park. Left to right: Valerie, James,Anne, Melanie, Althea, Marie Louise, Elizabeth, Butsie and Billy Guste

Knott's Berry Farm 1966. Standing: Randy, Left to right: Valerie, Billy, Marie Louise, Melanie, Anne, James, Althea, Butsie (Mom) and Elizabeth.

Dorothy Schutten Guste celebrating her 97th birthday with Anne D. Guste, author of Stories of My Mother and The General's Cookbook" and Marie Louise Guste Nix.

CHAPTER NINE

In the Cathedral of Our Lady of Quadalupe, a diverse and faith-filled congregation stood on a cement floor speaking out loud with God, sometimes breaking into music. There were sounds of praise and thanksgiving blending with pleas in supplication and moans of sorrow. Flickering candles glowed warmly before little altars on either side of the nave. With arms raised to heaven, ladies swayed together, their wavy colorful skirts blending into one another. After Mass, Alfredo led us around the sanctuary as he explained the story of the Virgin's appearances to Juan Diego and how her image had miraculously appeared on his cloak. We stopped to behold this venerable image flanked by crutches of those who came with infirmities and left free of them.

An undeniable Spirit swept over me. God touched down. Worship was redefined in this experience, and it wasn't a thing you do on Sunday. It was a sense of awe in the Presence of the Divine. The passionate fervor in the midst of all this closeness changed me.

At breakfast Alfredo told us our day would start with a luxury float through opulent fresh foliage draped with colorful tropical flowers. It would be a bullfight after that.

My sisters and I quietly looked into a muddy lagoon while Alfredo paid for the tickets to the floating gardens. The park was abandoned, except for two sleepy overfed attendants plopped on stools and leaning on the ticket house. A once colorful gondola rounded the corner of a vegetated island. The dock attendant pulled the little vessel in and a matronly woman with a paisley scarf tied under her chin climbed out, holding the hand of a little boy.

"What a joke!" cheered Jimmy. "You call this romantic?" Another canoe floated into view carrying a young couple who couldn't be distracted even by the noise-makers.

"It looks like someone feels differently, Jim." Mom smiled sheepishly looking over in their direction.

"Am I color-blind, or do the boats look completely faded to you?" I asked Melanie and pulled out the postcard from my notebook. Our bawdy bunch boarded the weather worn vessel, Alfredo took charge of untying knots to disengage from the dock and we began a leisurely winding float through some droopy gardens. Giggles turned to cackling, hooting and hollering and we held on for dear life to the rims of that rocking gondola.

After the ride, as we traipsed through the parking lot, an anxious caballero cornered Dad. "Buenos dias, Senor!" he said as he shook out a gigantic heavy black cape.

"Hey, my friend, could you possibly watch the way you shake out that thing?" Mom jumped into the car to avoid the minor dust storm, slammed the door and shook off her blouse.

Dad became interested in the black cape.

"Butsie, have a look at this fantastic cape! The boys would love it, wouldn't they?"

"We can do without that! Billy!"

"This cape makes a costume for hundreds of characters. Take a look and tell me—what do you think?" Mother flipped the visor down and flipped it up again. She found the fan, and beat hard.

"I told you what I think. Let's go. The children need some lunch."

"How many pesos, Senor?" The vendor announced his price and Dad quickly retorted, "I can't afford it."

"Senor, then for you..." He came back with a new and lower price.

"I still can't afford it." He pointed into the car. "You see the kids I have in there?"

"Si, Senor, then only for you, you can have it for..."

"That's a deal!"

Alfredo looked at Mom and tipped his head. He sent a smile her way then moved to the flower cart nearby. He came back with a crimson rose, stepped near her window and knelt to present it.

"Por la bella Senora!" he smiled brightly and handed the rose to Mom.

"When do we go ahead and tell him off?" Jimmy called.

"He's being sweet." Mel said.

"He is flirting with Mom and I've had it." Allie said.

"Not even four feet away from Dad, too!" Jimmy kept up.

Mother sent back a cozy sort of smile. "Alfredo is only being nice. He is a very kind gentleman, and we ought to be grateful to him for putting up with us all week. You're a good sport, Alfredo, I've got to give it to you!" She smiled appreciatively.

Dad pitched his package to the rear. Alfredo pulled out of the parking lot and headed to his favorite lunch shop near there.

"I'll stick to plain eggs and toast, please." Mom stepped down the hall and went in the door marked "Damas."

During lunch, Alfredo talked about bullfights and today's hero.

"Best of all, I managed to get some very special box seats, por la senora." He smiled victoriously at Mom. 'You will have the best view of anybody for a very special bullfight!" His white teeth were enormous when he smiled.

"I'll go powder my nose." Mom said. I followed her out. In the bathroom, we strategized.

"What do we do? I can't imagine watching a bullfight from ringside seats. I'm the one who was scared at the circus, when the lions came out. I can't do this." Animal nightmares haunted me as a child. Large dogs popped up in my dreams appearing near the foot of my bed. In another dream an elephant escaped from the zoo and charged down our block.

Mom and I got up a game plan. As soon as everyone was wrapped up in the bullfight and their popcorn, we'd sneak to the back row and wait for it to be over. At the table, Alfredo had the troop captivated and psyched up.

"Mom, we got box seats for the bullfight! What a gas! Wait till Billy and Randy hear about this!" Jim cheered.

"You have the best seats in the entire ring!" Alfredo beamed. Mom and I looked at one another and gulped. She winked at me.

"It won't be too bad, Mom." I slipped accidentally.

"What do you mean, won't be too bad? We got the best seats in the house!" Dad said, as if he didn't believe his ears.

It was a scorching afternoon for man to conquer beast and a jostling boisterous crowd filled the stadium. I trudged into the box behind the others. All this closeness was heating up.

"Does the bull ever escape from the ring, Alfredo?" Melanie asked.

"Hardly ever." He replied. Althea started crying, huddling near Mother.

"Be a sport, Allie. Let's think positive."

Alfredo enthusiastically pointed out the Chapel where the Matador prayed and said that the brave soul would momentarily prance out into the ring and meet his lady to get her blessing. Alfredo explained how they butchered the meat immediately following the fight. Mother gulped and looked heavenward.

At the clang of cymbals the crowd rose and fell silent. A brass band struck up the national anthem and proud voices belted out the chorus. Wild cheering began as the tiny matador emerged from a door across the stadium to the far right. The beast he intended to outwit busted out of a stall on the left and I threw my head over my knees. The broad black animal, built like a mack truck, charged clear across the field before I could blink. I clutched Mother's leg and she took my arm. The crowd around us jumped up and down screaming and yelling, and vendors shouted "co-cah." I held my head in my hands, staring at peanut shells on the cement floor, remembering to keep my eyes open and breathe deep. A shower of popcorn puffs poured over my head. Men in guayabera shirts mopped their foreheads between their cheers. The ladies in embroidered dresses fanned themselves furiously while gabbing and chattering non-stop. Peeking out through my fingers I caught sight of the crimson blood running down the side of a velvet black beast as he fell to the ground.

"You look white as a ghost." Mother said to me.

"Let's get a coke and some popcorn." Dad suggested.

"Great idea! Said Jim, waving down the vendor.

"I'd better take her to the back of the stadium." Mother said.

"Well, if you think it's necessary. But we have box seats! Come back when she's feeling a little better." Dad replied.

"Thank you."

The Marine's song, God Bless America, America the Beautiful. Dad's song fest after the bullfight was coincidentally patriotic. I wondered if he had felt a little grossed out at the bullfight too.

"We live in the greatest country of the world kids. Blessed by God in every way. You're growing up in a country of abundance and material blessings."

"What's that mean, Dad?" asked Jim.

"We have natural resources – land, water, energy sources. We have a form of government which allows us to develop those resources to the fullest. That's why we've become the strongest nation in the world."

"Really?"

"We need to stay strong to protect our freedom. Our country is only as strong as we are, kids. That's why I don't let any of you talk about foolish fears. I want to make men out of all of you! In unity there is strength!"

"But, Dad, most of us are girls!" I complained.

"That's not what I'm talking about, Marie Louise. I'm talking about having character and true conviction—living according to principles, and giving everything you've got to make the world a better place. I mean I want you to have real strength and true grit. And that comes from your own will. It's a decision. That's what I mean when I say I want to make men out of all of you."

"Well, it would be just as meaningful to me I you said you'd like to make strong people out of us all, Dad." I replied.

"Yes. Billy really! I'm a woman and I'm glad no one tried to make a man out of me." Said Mom innocently.

"You know what I'm getting at."

"Sorry to disappoint you Dad," I said.

"Disappoint me?" You could never disappoint me! I'm so proud of each of you. I can taste it!"

"I'm hot" someone popped up.

"I don't think the air conditioner's working." said Allie. "I've been hot all during this lecture."

"If everybody's hot, turn off the air and roll the windows down. Spread out." Said Dad.

"Put your head close to the window and breathe some fresh air, children."

"Fresh air? It's hot as blazers and dusty, too, Mom!" I said.

"It's healthy. There's nothing like fresh air."

"But this isn't fresh air, Mom." I said.

"Just breathe it. All these Mexicans are doing fine on it. I bet they don't have air conditioners in their cars." Replied Mother.

"You've got a point Mom."

"We're not Mexicans, Mom. We're Americans!" said Mel.

"That's the beauty of traveling." Said Dad. "The air conditioner breaks down when we're traveling in Texas too." Said Dad.

"At least we have American air in Texas." Said Allie. "It doesn't stink." she said wincing. "It's disgusting!"

"Who has diarrhea?" said Jim.

"Not me." Chimed in several voices.

"I have to go to the bathroom," said Val. "Can we stop soon?"

"We'll stop as soon as we can. I promise, Val!" Dad said consolingly.

"Everyone look for your shoes and comb your hair." Said Mother.

CHAPTER TEN

"Is this the road to Acapulco?" Dad leaned out the window to ask a passerby. I heard him and sprang up to forage for the map.

"We agreed not to get directions from kids on the street." Mom put in.

"Then read the map, please."

"I'll tell you what. Give me the wheel and you read it to me." She replied.

We gazed out at dappled cattle growing up healthy on the plains.

"Look at that farmland!" Dad said, pointing.

"Farmland? Will you please look at the road?" Mom yelped. A few passengers bounced into upright position to keep an eye out.

He found a spot to pull over. A Pemex 100 truck whizzed by.

"Whew! That was a wide load! Close call, Daddeo." Jimmy called out.

"Isn't it your turn to drive, Mom?" Anne asked. Dad stayed silent with a funny look on his face. He pulled over on a shoulder of the road.

On the road in the passenger seat, he started in with some encouragement about what we were doing. I wonder if he was reminding himself. “There’s no better way to expand your horizons than to travel in a different country.”

“When are we stopping next, Dad?” Valerie asked timidly.

“Stopping? Are you joking? Listen to this, Butz. Is it a new sense of humor? We aren’t ten miles outside Mexico City and someone wants to stop! Who asked about stopping?” Dad called out. Val put her head down.

“The only bathroom I know of between here and Acapulco was back there. We’re not stopping, does everyone get it?” He asked. “Anyone who needs to go to the bathroom, just remember Queen Elizabeth and you’ll grow through discipline!”

“Did Queen Elizabeth ever get Montezuma’s revenge?” Val asked.

“Val looked green. “Do you have Kaopectate tucked someplace?” I said.

“Val’s been up all night, Billy. She didn’t tell anyone. We better find a bathroom quick, and I mean business. This is no joke.” Mom said.

“At least get over to the window, Valerie!” Mel said.

“I’m getting in the back.” Said Jimmy.

"Valerie, your face looks grey!" Allie stammered. Val's eyes bulged and she held her waist.

"I'm not really sick. I never get sick. It's just my stomach." Val said.

"Oh just that. Your stomach. Who are you kidding? We know what it is, Val." Said Jimmy. "You're embarrassed."

The Pemex station loomed up ahead, and it was busy. Val disappeared into the ladies bathroom. When ten minutes had passed and Val was still in there, everyone quieted down.

"Alright in there, Val?" I called.

"I'll be out any minute." She called back.

"Sure you're okay?" I called.

"Yeah, I'll be out." She sounded weak.

In the wagon, Mother insisted everyone quit the jokes. "At least it wasn't that stupid claustrophobia of hers." Jimmy said.

"Don't even talk about imaginary diseases. It's foolishness. You can't let fears and phobias control you. You need to control them!" Dad said.

Valerie limped back and climbed into the wagon. "Glad you made it back, Val." Allie said.

"Everyone was worried about you. Are you okay?" Mel asked.

"It's about time. I was hot as blazers in this car." Anne said.

"Everything come out alright?" Liz asked. Mom glared at her.

"We thought you fell in." Dad said.

"Valerie come sit in the front. This has gone too far!" Mom said. Mom began to spoon Coke to her a teaspoon at a time.

"Butsie, about this station wagon. Each morning I ought to check into the Ford dealership wherever we are. I got a list of the dealers back in Mexico City." Dad said.

"That was smart. Thanks." She responded.

"In Acapulco, we're resting up. Just going to the beach and we'll enjoy the hotel. We don't have to do much touring around." Dad said.

"Wow, I never heard you say anything like that before Dad." Melanie said.

"How will we learn anything?" Jimmy said with tongue in cheek.

I avoided looking at Val while we prayed the Rosary. I wanted to keep from thinking about that bug. After the chanting was over, Mom turned Val's chin to her.

"Feeling better now?" She asked. "You look better."

"Must have been those tacos and the claustrophobia too." Val said.

"Don't talk about phobias. I'm making men of character out of you." Dad said firmly. Some bickering started up about who the window belonged to.

"Doesn't seem like the Rosary did much to help. The kids are going bananas over a stupid window." Mel said. "You can stop them, Dad!" Melanie complained.

"Your Dad has a lot to think about. He didn't even hear it." Mom said. "He's probably preparing a Commencement Address."

"Really? Dad, is that true?" Mel asked.

"Sometimes I do develop ideas for speeches while we're going down the highway. I jot them down when we stop." He answered.

"You're going to speak at a Commencement soon?" I asked. "I hadn't heard a thing about it."

"Every so often I am asked to do it, Marie. The Commencements this year are over." He said.

"You children don't know half of what your father does. Your Dad is a very important person. He's an excellent speaker and often gives the keynote address. He is a real leader I can promise you that." Mom said. "You can learn a lot if you listen to him."

"Oh." Allie said. "I had no idea Dad could do that."

"He lectures to us a lot. I hope he doesn't say the same stuff. I'm not sure it would work too well." Jimmy said. "If we don't want to listen, why would they?"

"Push over, I told you already, Jimmy. You're hogging the seat!" Anne fumed. "I was explaining why your father gets lost in thought. He can't solve squabbles all the time. Let your Dad think, alright? Work it out without fighting." Mom said.

"One thing we can do is quit getting souvenirs that crowd up the car." Dad said.

"We should try not to look at peddlers." Mom added. Soon as the words escaped her lips we careened into a little village open air market and Mom gaped at an open air boutique overflowing with colorful lamps hanging from the tarpaulin, shaped like various fruits. She gasped. "They're gorgeous!" She was out the car before the protest broke out, picking a couple of lamps for the old oak tree.

"Lord help!" Val squealed as the dark hefty fellow stuck his head in the wagon looking for a spot to deposit the new cargo.

"It's only three, and they're wrapped really well. Prop the pillows near them."

"Rest time." Dad announced.

Thirty minutes into quiet time, I gingerly brought it up. “Montezuma’s revenge is real. I don’t believe I’m coming back here voluntarily.”

“Don’t let it get you. It’s a choice. The food’s delicious!” Dad said.

“Maybe you have an iron stomach or your shot worked better. Have you even gotten that bug?” I asked.

“Had it every day since we crossed the border.” He replied.

“You never say anything about it, and you eat everything they serve.”

“A parent needs to keep some things quiet.”

“But why keep eating guacamole, tacos, and enchiladas every night?

“Because it’s delicious!” He answered, smiling. Who cares if it gives you a little stomach trouble? It’s probably good for your system!”

“You have a positive attitude on being sick? It seems impossible!” I said indignantly.

“Keep your chin up. It’s all in the way you look at things. Decide to be optimistic about anything that happens to you.” He continued.

“It’s unreal.”

“Call it anything you want. If it works for me, it’ll work for you, too, honey.”

"Do you ever feel like you're in a bad mood? I mean, kind of depressed?" I asked.

"Definitely not. And don't talk about anything like that in front of children. It's like phobias. If it crosses your mind, don't give it power over you." He explained. "Change what you're doing. Get some exercise. Get busy doing something. Get into a project. Clean something and you'll forget all about being depressed. If you're ever down in the dumps come to me. I'll give you a project that'll keep you busy the whole afternoon." He offered.

"Sounds like fun." I said skeptically.

"Fun or not, it works! And if something works, use it." He sang out.

"Doing math homework makes me feel less depressed sometimes. I hate math, but I find it so hard to do it that it makes me forget my problems."

"What are your problems, anyway? Seems to me you're doing pretty well. Your grades are great, you're healthy, you look pretty, what's your problem?" he asked puzzled.

"Billy tells me the same thing. That I don't have any problems. I even agreed with him last time he gave me that talk." I admitted.

"Well, then its obvious. You just give in to feelings. Don't let it get you." He said. Even though it was hard, I knew it was mostly true. It was good to know that common sense could help.

"I have one problem I can't get rid of, Dad. It's you. Constant optimism just isn't for real. I feel sick. Can we stop at a gas station?" I bent over.

"We'll be getting to one. Did you say I made you sick?" he asked.

"I don't think so. Uh..." I stammered.

Acapulco. An Eden-like oasis after the cactus-dotted desert. A dreamy place to drink in the summer sun near the crystal clear aquamarine waters of the Pacific ocean. While our little troop basked in the glorious ocean waves, Dad made friends in the service department in the Ford dealership.

When they told him the old white wagon needed a new battery, flying the family home seemed an expensive alternative. Dad decided to trust the caballeros in there and bump up his Spanish. He would get plenty more opportunities to use it over the open hood examining the car engine in the heat.

The tour guide Mother hired brought us by the romantic Las Brisas resort which offered luxury suites for honeymooning couples with hot tubs overlooking the Atlantic.

"Imagine being stuck in a place like this with a girl, and nothing to do but swim, eat and look at each other! What a bore! It'd be worse than this trip!" Jimmy said.

"Aren't you having fun?" Mother sounded as though she were shocked.

"I think it would be a total bore to be stuck in one of these apartments with your wife and call that a honeymoon. What's there to do? Anyway, I hate girls." He said.

"Don't say 'hate' Jimmy. Thank you." Came Mom. "When people get married they want to spend a lot of time together and talk. Just <u>be</u> together."

"Just be together. Yecch." He said.

That evening we went to a nightclub atop a ritzy hotel to watch young men taking graceful daring dives into choppy waves off the cliffs lining the ocean. The cliffs outside the panoramic window were lit up and thick white waves crashed one after the next on the jagged rocks below. The sight of that raging ocean from the vantage point atop the cliff and the very thought of divers flying through the air gave me goosebumps in advance for these brave men. The show began, drums introduced each one and their sleek bodies sailed gracefully through the night air to enter the rumbling ocean. It was a breathtaking display of courage and competence which would remain forever implanted in my mind.

The spectacle was almost worth the trip.

"Can you believe anyone could get up the courage to do it? I said. "I couldn't get myself to go off the high diving board in the pool today!"

"Chicken!" Jimmy reproached.

“How could anyone be so brave? Can anyone explain this to me? How could they get themselves to do it?” I kept asking.

“It’s a matter of training.” Dad explained. “They’ve probably been training to do this all their life.”

“There’s a fine line between heroes and fools sometimes.” Mother remarked dreamily, sighing.

“Your Mother’s mighty brave, Marie Louise. She had ten children.” Dad said.

“Stop that, Billy. You know having a child is the healthiest thing in the world for a woman!”

“You know,” Dad continued. “Every time we had a child we had prayed for one. But you never know what you’ll get when you have children. We were lucky. And we love each of you. Each of you couldn’t be more perfect. We’ve had good luck. But it takes bravery. You have to take risks in life or you’ll never get anything out of it. You have to stick your neck out and try things, you have to be prepared to fail, get hurt, and be disappointed. It’s part of life. Everyone has to be as brave as these divers some time in life, and take a risk.”

“It’s true, Billy.” She turned to look at him and raised her glass for a toast.

“I have been the luckiest man in the world.” He beamed at Mother.

Next day was for sun, sand, tiki bar, naps and dress for dinner in best shorts.

According to Mom, we wouldn't say that we were going out to "eat" dinner, we would go and "have" dinner. She often had a "nicer" way of saying things.

La Riviera, a four-star haute-gourmet restaurant and nightclub was generally for adults only, a place for romance, such as when you were going to get engaged, or for when you made it to the big time.

There were some flickering gas lamps on either side of a well polished door with a brass handle. A menu was mounted in a shadow box on the white stucco wall.

"This looks lovely, Billy. I hope they let us in." Mother reflected casting a glance around at her group. Dad had white buck shoes on. He had brought them for the meeting. The coat he had left at the hotel. The sign read "Coat and Tie Required."

"They must want coats and ties if they'd put it out here in English." I remarked.

"Well let's see if they'll make an exception for us. Remember I always say—where there's a will..."

The door opened and the perfect-postured Maitre D'hotel greeted us with a serious look. Right away Dad would have to do some begging or bargaining. "You children wait over there while I discuss things with this gentleman."

A few minutes later we were escorted through the main dining room towards a spiral staircase by the defeated Maitre D'. The place was filled with dreamy honeymooners and an aristocratic looking crowd. We wound our way up the staircase to a second floor where a pianist in a tuxedo was seated erect sending strains of romantic melodies to the diners downstairs.

"Perfect for us! We won't disturb anyone." Dad followed the Maitre D' to a long rectangular table near a picture window fronting the street. There were small candelabras on either end of the table and a couple of bouquets of fresh cut flowers, too. Dad looked over the menu and announce that we were splitting orders of steak.

"Don't worry, Butz." Dad said as she started to object. He placed his hand over hers and returned to the menu.

The waiter was of course peeved but scratched his head and looked the other way.

"Now where is the wine list?" Dad asked. The guy opened his mouth as if to speak but couldn't figure out what to say. "Si, Senor." He went to grab a wine list.

"Can I help you choose, sir?" he asked condescendingly.

"Maybe so. What do you recommend?" The waiter pointed to a lower-priced bottle of red table wine.

Dad ignored that and continued his study of the list while the guy shifted his weight preparing to write it down. He at last pointed to a special vintage of Burgundy. The guy suppressed a little cough. "Si Senor." He shuffled off.

"I guess he didn't think you knew a thing about wine, Dad! He didn't even want to bring you the list!" I mentioned.

"A good bottle of wine is worth a little extra." He commented as he began getting ready for a raffle game. He tore up a napkin and put a number on each piece and threw them in a wine glass. tearing up pieces of a cocktail napkin to number and put in a glass.

The waiter showed up with the wine and from this point forward pretended not to see anyone he was dealing with. He poured a sip for Dad to approve, then poured Mom's.

"What was his problem?" Jimmy said. "Does anyone at this table have B.O.?"

"Yeah,—Valerie!" Liz pulled through for everyone.

"What's that song you all sing about 'Elegance' Allie? It's from 'Hello Dolly.' Mother asked, her white handkerchief at her nose, catching a breath between chuckles.

"The one about Barnaby and Cornelius?" Allie said.

"Yes. I want you to do that number for me back at the hotel." Mom said.

The steaks arrived. "Who gets these, sir?" Dad pointed out the recipients. Extra little plates had to be asked for.

Dad asked for a round of "The Great Amen" and I cringed. "Oh, no—not that!" was the general response.

"Just one round. Come on everybody, join hands! 'Amen. Amen. Amen Amen, Amen. Wonderful." He moved on to cutting up the steaks.

"I thought we were getting away from it all—even from Father Romagosa." Jimmy complained.

Back in our suite at the Acapulco Hilton Mother remembered to ask for the song and dance from Dolly. The girls had it down to a tee:

Yes New York, it's really us

Barnaby and Cornelius

All the guests of Mr. Hackle are

Feeling great and look spectacular

What a knack, there is to that

Acting like a born aristocrat

We've got elegance,

if you ain't got elegance,

You can never ever carry...if off!

CHAPTER ELEVEN

The Road Home

"Who clobbered me on the shoulder?" Valerie was hot as a pistol.

"Jimmy's foot. He was doing handstands in the back seat." Anne reported.

"Liar." Jimmy poked a finger in Anne's rib.

"Not." Anne defended.

"I am so squinched in here I could die." Val said.

"Dad says 'Don't leave to tomorrow what you could do today.'" Mel said.

"We're bored!" Said Elizabeth.

"Only boring people get bored." Dad's index finger shot up.

"You're not a bore, Liz, you're a pimple-face frizz-ball!" said Jim.

"And Marie's a cheeseball." I gave him an icy stare.

"It's those cheesy pink sunglasses you bought for 99 cents at Woolworths." Mel added.

"They're a good fake. Gus Mayer had a pair just like them for $10!"

"Time for a song-fest, everyone! How about *Zippededooda*!" Dad switched the subject.

Zippedee-dooda, Zippedee-ay

My oh my what a wonderful day!

Plenty o' sunshine going my way.

Wonderful feeling, wonderful day!

"Great!" Dad index finger went up again. "*Oh What a Beautiful Morning!*"

O what a beautiful morning.

O what a beautiful day!

I've got a beautiful feeling,

Everything's going my way!

"'When the Saints Go Marching In'".

O when the Saints go marchin' in,

O when the Saints go marchin' in,

O how I want to be in that number,

When the saints go marchin' in.

"Sunshine!"

So let the sunshine in, face it with a grin

Smilers never lose and frowners never win....

“Seventy- Six Trombones, Oh Susanna, Do-Re-Me.

“You’ve changed colors Marie. You were white, now you’re greyish green.” Allie said.

“I’ll get in the back and take care of whoever feels sick.” Mom said.

“It’s a new day.” Dad said taking off on the road again. “What’s on your mind, Marie?” Dad inquired.

“About the pioneer spirit and our mission to build a country where there’s liberty, justice and security for all.” I said.

“Yes...and...?”

“We had a hero in John F. Kennedy. We had a President who wanted it all—justice, equality and a better life for every American. Look what happened to him! A madman took charge of the nation’s history and shot him dead one sunny day. It’s depressing, really depressing.” I moaned.

“Marie, they killed his body, but they can never kill his spirit. His spirit is immortal, and lives on in all who loved him. When a hero dies, it falls to others to carry on his work.” Dad said.

“You have the answer to everything, Dad. It makes sense when you say it, but later I feel confused again.”

“If you feel confused, come to me. I’ll explain it again.”

"The world is different than the one you and Mother grew up in. There's so much violence and crime...and assassinations and hi-jacking. The world has so many problems now."

"Marie Louise, you don't know this so I have to tell you. You're growing up in one of the sunniest and best times in the history of America. Several years before you were born everyone had come home from war. Our country emerged victorious. You grew up in a victory celebration. When the world is at war – you have real problems. A lot of suffering, struggling and people losing loved ones. It's a survival fight. Sure, we've had some catastrophes in your lifetime. But we're living in the best of times, sweetie. I don't want to upset you, or make you feel worse, but you really need to know the truth."

"I see what you mean." I slumped down.

I wondered whether my parent's satisfaction and joy in life was a chosen practice, a skill, a studied art? Or was it a pure gift of grace, unfair bounty bestowed on the two of them to last forever? The answer came soon enough.

"Hey, Dad. What's this book you're reading?" Melanie paged through the volume she picked up off the floor. "*Ten Days to a Great New Life.*"

"That's a book I'm reading to get ideas on how I can improve myself and my life, get more out of it, and get my goals accomplished." Dad answered.

"I can't believe you'd read anything like that! You seem completely fulfilled, completely happy. You always have all the answers. Why would you read anything like that!" Melanie was dumbfounded.

"I can hardly believe you want your life to get any better! You never have problems. How come you want to read something like that?" I queried.

"I'm always working to improve myself and get more out of life by putting more into it. This book sets out a plan for improving your life by setting goals and making a schedule for attaining your goals. It's great!"

"I thought you had all the answers already." I said.

"I've been around a while, so I've had time to learn. I like to pretend I'm still 29 but I'm not."

"That's thinking positive." Came Mom from the back seat.

"When you're in the stage of life your Mom and I are in, you start to feel as if you're beginning to understand things. You start to have some of the answers to things you've been wondering all along. It's great."

"Wonderful." Mom joined in with dry wit.

"Yes, life begins at 40!" Dad repeated.

"Great. Where does that leave me?" Melanie asked.

"You're young. You've got questions, feelings, thoughts—that's wonderful!"

"But we need some answers." I moaned.

"They come with age and time, honey. I've made mistakes. I've learned a lot from them. There are some things everybody's got to learn on their own."

"Shove over, Althea." Jimmy heaved her leftward.

"Cool your jets, Jimmy." Valerie hurled him a dictatorial glance.

"I'm hot and she's hogging the seat." He answered.

"Time for *Ramblin' Rose*!" Dad called out.

"I hate that song!" I said.

Rambling rose, rambling rose!

Why you ramble, no one knows!

Wild and windblown,

That's how you've grown.

Who can cling to... a rambling rose?

"*Volare!*" Dad called.

"Not that. Please!"

"I'm bored!" Valerie complained.

"Only boring people get bored." Mel quipped. "Take a nap."

"Know-it-all." Valerie added.

I opened up Ten days to a Great New Life. Some of the day schedule charts were filled in. I started to feel sick.

"Marie, you look white!" Mother said looking back at me.

"A minute ago she was green. She's better." Jimmy guffawed.

"Cut it out, Jimmy." Mother gave him a look in the rearview mirror.

"My stomach's about to explode! I implored.

"Gas station. Gas station. Coming up." Mother looked all around on her way into the main drag.

"St. Anthony. Where are you?" said Allie.

"Whew. I see a Pemex Station. Pull in! Dad careened into the station taking a wide turn and jerked to a stop in front of the pumps. "Everybody out."

"Pee-you." Howled Liz.

"What?" Mother asked.

"I said pee-you. Roll down your window and take a whiff. Yikes."

"You're lucky the air conditioner's been working all this time, so you haven't smelled a thing for a while. Well go on, Marie." I hesitated to climb out in case moving made my stomach explode. Slowly I scooched my way out of the car. It was a superbad place to stop. The stench, the dirty toilet, the air thick and putrid nearly knocked me out. Returning to the company I was wiped out. I expected laughs."

"Oh no, you look awful." Mom announced she needed to get in back and help me out.

"It's alright. Really. Nothing we all haven't had by now." Mom knew by the looks of me that this was worse than the usual. In Mexico you were either sick or drastically sick. This was the drastically sick variety. She came back and began spooning me Kaopectate first, then Coke every five minutes. It seemed like hours, but eventually my equilibrium returned.

"Here's a game." Dad popped. "Everybody say something nice to the person sitting next to you."

"Oh, no." Jimmy was sitting near Elizabeth. He tried. "Your hair doesn't look as bad today as it did yesterday. What happened?"

"I combed it. You don't have hair. So you don't need to comb it." She replied.

"Melanie doesn't stink today." Said Val.

"Next?" Dad led the game.

"Allie, you look bee-you-ti-ful. Especially since you let me have the window." Cheeped Elizabeth.

"Marie Louise doesn't look cool like usual. That's a compliment." Came Anne.

"Yes, Anne. Beauty comes from within. When you doing something for others you're beautiful, and it doesn't matter what you look like." Mom put in. "Up to a point, that is. You need to think about it a little bit."

"Let's hear a round of Let the Sun Shine in. Then came Pack Up Your Troubles, She'll be Comin' round the Mountain, On Top of Old Smokey, I've Been Working on a Railroad, Yankee Doodle Dandy, This land, My Country Tis of Thee, Happy Trails To You.

"It's happy trails to this station wagon when we get home." Val laughed.

"This station wagon was fine until you had two martinis that night in Mexico City and rammed it up on that curb!" Mom told Dad.

"I'll be darned. I'm not the one to blame." Dad chortled.

"Val, I think you mean IF we get back home to New Orleans. We're not back yet."

Dusk fell on another day of wheeling it northward, dreaming of reaching the border before dark. I conjured ramming into a stray buffalo, or meeting up with bandits.

"Looks like we're driving at night in Mexico, eh Dad?" Jimmy asked.

"I thought we'd be in Saltillo by now. I'm going slower. We've been having some generator problems." He answered.

"Hope we don't run into any mountains." Mel added. "I'll never forget that nightmare riding into Quanajuato. That was one of the worst nights of my life."

"We'll be in Saltillo, shortly, kids. I'm sure of it!" Mom said.

There was a flapping sound atop the wagon.

Dad stopped on the side of the road and tightened up the ropes securing the luggage on top the car. When he put the brakes on, a slim paperback book slid out from under his seat. It was *How to Stop Worrying and Start Living* by Norman Vincent Peale.

Opening it up, my eyes fell on an appropriate passage. "Shut out the past from your mind, and refuse to carry the load of tomorrow." It sounded interesting. "This says the best way to prepare for tomorrow is to concentrate with all your intelligence on doing today's work superbly. 'How to Stop Worrying and Start...'"

"Hey, Marie, get out and give me a hand!" Dad called.

When he revved up the engine we talked about it.

"I read that book many years ago and the wisdom I gained from it has always stuck with me!" Dad said. "You'd like it and you'd profit from it if you'd practice what he has to say." He told me.

"Really?" I said.

"Yes, really. It's about positive thinking and positive attitudes. We can conquer all our problems if we think positive."

"You brought this to read on the trip, Dad?"

"I brought it to review. I learned the principles long ago—never to allow yourself to worry. It's a waste of mental energy."

The town of Saltillo seemed deserted. There didn't appear to be a single traffic light The map made it look like a reasonable stop. Nothing resembled a hotel. Dad pulled to a stop in front of a small stucco building with a light on near the door. We hoped it might be an eating establishment. It was unadorned, stripped except for a primitive sign hanging out.

"Oh boy, this looks great!" Came Jim.

"Did we have to stop here, Mom?" Melanie asked after Dad had climbed out. Mother took a pause and calmly replied—"It could be worse!"

Dad returned. "Good news—we won't starve."

Inside was as dull as outside. An eerie feeling of traveling to still yet another foreign country surrounded a quiet group. Not a picture on the walls, no rug, tablecloth, curtain, only tables and chairs inside a bare room. Empty. Strange. Clean however.

A man came over and assisted my father in putting two tables together. No meanness came from him. Nor cheer.

"This shows us how lucky we are. It's a good lesson for us to have a taste of life as others live it. We're spoiled." Mom said.

"It makes me realize how much we take for granted." I added.

The owner-chef-cashier-attendant and cook came over to tell us what he would be able to serve us for dinner.

"Bring it on out." Dad said jovially. When the dinner was on, the man pulled up a chair and sat down, leaning on another chair to talk. He had some rooms we hadn't noticed in the back. A tiny establishment of perhaps eight rooms in all. Before the meal was over, Dad had checked us in.

The man led us to the back to show us our rooms. They were spacious and each room had two twin beds. There was something missing. Almost everything was missing. The same thick musty odor filled the air in each of them. It would be a roof, but that was about it. The kids went from room to room checking to see was there anything better in the next room.

"I think we need three rooms since there are only two twin beds in each room." Dad said.

"Two rooms will be enough." I said. I knew that Mel and I would be the ones to stay in the room farthest from Dad and Mom's door.

"Let's stay close to each other in a place like this. It's scary."

"If we can have rollaway beds, we can stay in two rooms." The man came with the beds, left linens on one of the beds, and bid us goodnight. The sheets he provided were made of heavy white pique.

"Could these be tablecloths?" Val asked.

"How are you supposed to get them to stay on? There are no corners!" Allie said.

"Make the best of it, girls. You've been to camp. It's not that bad." Dad was weary.

"Look at the towels!" Elizabeth cackled. "How are we going to dry ourselves with these, I'd like to know?"

"Elizabeth, perhaps we can wait till tomorrow night to take showers and baths." Mother commented. She looked around, took some breaths and went in her adjoining room. At the door, she turned to us.

"Now don't go and tell everyone your parents make you jam in one room and share beds, please. You all decided you wanted to all stay in one room, right?" Mother said.

"Right, Mom." I replied. "We're fine."

Dad opened the door bringing in warm currents of night air. Cattle lowing in the neighborhood was something like music and the quiet country peace remarkable.

"God is good to us, kids." He smiled. "We better thank Him!"

"Like Mom always said, it could be worse!" Valerie went over and stood near Dad. "What's that big round thing over there, Dad?" She asked pointing to a cylindrical tank. "What a place for an oil tank!"

"I'm not sure what it is Val. It sure does smell bad around here!" Dad said. For a moment, there was a hush. Dad had broken his golden rule. His students began laughing uncontrollably.

"Really Dad? What happened to positive thinking?" Jimmy asked breaking into laughter.

"It's a good experience for you kids!" Dad laughed and joined the foolishness. "It's going to make pioneer men and women out of you!"

"I'm so excited." Said Liz. Dad had a final admonition before the group turned in.

"I want silence after we say goodnight. Everyone go to sleep. We need a good night's rest. Do you understand me?" He passed a look around.

"Promise, Dad. I'll keep everyone quiet." I assured him.

Despite the plan for peace and quiet, Jimmy went in the bathroom time after time, climbing over Valerie and Althea's bed repeatedly. Dad appeared at the door.

"What is all the noise? I told you I want quiet in here." He said.

"Jimmy isn't feeling well." I explained in defense.

"What's the matter, Jimmy?"

"I have a stomach-ache."

"Okay then, when you have to use the bathroom, don't flush the toilet."

"I have to flush the toilet."

"Then do it quietly!" He said gravely and then disappeared. Chuckles broke out. "I said, quiet!" Came Dad from the other room. Silence. I lay awake holding Anne in my arms in a twin bed.

At two or three a.m. there was the crunch of tires rolling over gravel outside the door and then an engine cut. Achy from tossing and turning, I heard Dad in the next room moving towards the door. The company was up instantly, alert, speculating, threatened. At the window, we grouped close to observe Dad out there in his pajamas, sharing old war stories with an American couple who had had similar experiences South of the Border. They were cackling and yacking like old friends, while Dad helped the man take his suitcases down from on top of their wagon.

"What's going on out there?" I asked.

"Just another family getting lost on the road in Mexico. They didn't think they'd land here, either. Go on back to sleep. We have a day's drive tomorrow, we should even make it across the border and back in to the States."

"None of us can sleep in here. Maybe it's the smell, I don't know." I said.

"Do your best, or you'll be tired tomorrow." He said.

In the morning our friend in the cafe gave us breakfast and directions to the Ford dealership. There was more in the town of Saltillo than we could see at night. The stop we made was south of town.

"Thank goodness there's a ford dealership here. The generator was heating up yesterday. I thought it might catch fire." Dad told Mom.

"You mean we have to spend the morning in the dealership? I was hoping to get back to the States today." Said Jimmy.

"I can't wait to get back, too." Said Elizabeth.

"Then go pack your things and let's clear out of here." Dad said.

Back in the room I sponged off with sticky yellow soap and the pique hand towel.

"You used the hand towel for a wash cloth, what are you going to dry off with?" Elizabeth asked.

"I'll just have to use one of those thick heavy sheets. So what? They have to wash them anyway." I replied.

"What a girl scout!" Valerie cheered.

"Come on everybody, let's get going!" Dad said, poking his head in through the door.

It would be as a two or three hour wait in the dealership—the generator had to be replaced.

"Next time they're going to tell us the car needs to be replaced!" I suggested.

"They say two or three hours, but you know how that goes. Let's find a better hotel and get settled."

"Absolutely not! Soon as we're finished here we're hitting the road, and we'll make it to Laredo after all. Think positive!" He said.

Emptying the candy and gum machines, re-reading comic books, playing tic-tac-toe. There was a long row of red leather chairs with chrome arms lined up. With the scout troop fanned out, I tried to relax.

Dad handled business then Senor Camillieri, the owner and his new best friend came over to meet us. Senor Camillieri had on a crisp white short sleeve shirt. A gentleman of medium height, he was clearly well-fed and had his straight black hair slicked back off his face. His hairdo seemed held in place with some Brylcreem. He had a broad smile and the gleaming eyes of someone who had succeeded in every department of life, a totally jovial, self-satisfied individual. A well- groomed mustache curled upwards over his good-boy dimples. His cheeks were smooth, shiny and fat, and his skin much paler than the average Mexican.

"Well, hello, children, it is so nice to meet the Guste family! I hear you have been having a very good time in our country!" Senor said.

It was indeed a special new friendship. Senor Camillieri became a self-appointed Chamber of Commerce for the day and decided we were his responsibility. We could have been visiting dignitaries for the way he treated us. Dad's friendliness at brought a reward in a return of cordiality. After a few conversations about our experiences, Senor Camillieri disappeared for a few moments. He returned even more buoyant than before. "I just called home. My wife and I would love to invite all of you out to our villa for lunch. It will be much better for the children to wait out there, and it seems like you need to see the good side of Mexico, Senor y Senora. How about coming out for lunch?" Mother checked Dad before responding. He smiled.

"It is wonderful of you to invite us, Senor, but won't this be a big surprise for your wife? We have a large group here, and we would hate to impose on her." Mother explained.

"Oh, not at all. It is no problem at all. We love to have company. We love people. It will be our pleasure to have you, I assure you."

"Well, how can we say no? We'd love to come, Senor Camillieri."

Senor drove Dad and a few of the gang and had his employee drive Mother and the rest of us. On the way over Mother voiced her thoughts about how Mrs. Camillieri was feeling about this. “I think I’d want to wring someone’s neck if Dad ever pulled this on me. A whole family for lunch when we don’t speak their language? I think I’ve made a mistake. The poor lady is probably furious by now. How could I do this to anyone?”

“Beggars can’t be choosers, Mother.” I said soberly.

“Beggars? What do you mean beggars?” She retorted indignantly.

“At this point, if someone invites us out to their home for lunch, we better go. The way our luck’s been running I think we ought to just be glad when anything good comes our way!”

“You’ve certainly got a point there.”

“Yeah, and I’m sick of sitting around in a dealership.” Said Liz. “I’m out of comics.”

“We’re getting hungry, too.” Melanie added. “It’ll be cool to get a good home-cooked meal and see how the Mexicans really do things.”

“I guess it is good luck. It goes to show you. We still seem like nice people to someone.” Mother passed the comb around the car.

That poor lady, as Mother had dubbed her on the way out, was not so poor. The driver from the dealership saw to it that the guests arrived on time for the noonday meal.

“People are definitely buying Fords in Saltillo.” Mel said as she laid her eyes on the hacienda. It was a villa sprawled out with gardens surrounding, then further out were green fields speckled with contented cattle.

Up the front steps on super-wide L-shaped porch there was lots of white-painted wrought iron furniture and a long rectangular table for dining outside. Senora Camillieri was dutifully cordial, comfortably in charge of the luncheon with her husband's friends. She was large-breasted and plump all over, and wore a ruffled low-cut floor-length dress. Her fair skin and jet-black hair tied behind her head looked aristocratic. Servants came in and out of the central hallway inside the house to deliver appetizers and to receive instructions concerning the meal. Senora Camillieri was as gracious as could be considering the fact that she spoke no English. Mother and the Senora smiled at one another sympathetically throughout the lunch and siesta hours, while Dad and Senor exchanged stories and information about our different cultures.

Senora Camillieri's teenage daughters kept watch over a crew of toddlers and grade-school children and each of us found a match among our adopting family's brood. Stretching to find ways to express ourselves, we devised some little games to play sitting in a circle on the porch. There was no air-conditioning inside the house and the front porch was the coolest place to relax with overhead fans circulating warm air.

Lunch emerged from the kitchen continuously for about two hours. Courses and courses of every Mexican dish one could imagine.

Plenty of antipasto – olives, celery, tomatoes, eggs, treats too numerous to mention. By the third course, it became a problem to continue dining to be polite. Mother non-verbally instructed us to keep eating and smiling as best we could. The first course of asparagus wrapped in ham was followed by red chili in tortilla bowls, then enchiladas and taco chips with several sauces. Then came the main course with meat and vegetables served on skewers. Then out came the white nougat candy, Mexican pastries and coffee.

Back at the dealership there were decisions to make. The Ford was supposedly 100% recovered, with a spanking new generator and a thorough tune up. It was three-thirty in the afternoon. The next stop would be Laredo, Texas, but that would be a four-hour drive.

"What time does the sun do down around here, Senor?"

"About 6:30." Said Senor Camillieri.

"Let's give it a try. There's no sense sitting here and waiting till tomorrow. We could make it to Laredo tonight. What do you say, gang?" Dad cheered expecting the affirmative.

"Remember the drive at night into Quanajuato?" Melanie commented.

"It was pretty wild, Dad. Sanborn's said not to drive at night in Mexico." I added.

"While we're sitting here talking it over we might be making time on the road. Come on.

You'll never get anywhere in this life if you can't think positive." He turned to Senor Camillieri and thanked him again for all the hospitality. Dad started up the engine.

"Think positive, gang! In four short hours we'll be in the United States. Let's have a round of '*God Bless America*!'"

God Bless America,

Land that I love

Stand beside her and guide her

Through the night with the light from above...

"I'm glad we decided to wing it, Dad. I can't wait to get back in to the United States!" said Jim.

"Goodbye to tacos and enchiladas." I cheered.

"Goodbye to refried beans." Mel added.

"Goodbye to guacamole." Dad put in.

"Goodbye to Montezuma's revenge." Althea sang.

"Goodbye to Pemex Stations and Ford dealerships." Liz added.

"Goodbye to roadside peddlers." Mom sighed.

"I can't wait to see some signs on the road again." Valerie commented.

"I can't wait for a MacDonald's hamburger!" said Elizabeth.

"I can't wait to get Stuckey's pralines." Anne chirped.

"I can't wait to stay in an American hotel." Melanie said relieved.

"Sounds like you all are more than ready to get back gang. I have to admit, Mom and I are ready to go home ourselves! You've been terrific troopers. You're becoming pioneer children, and I'm mighty proud of you kids. I'm going to make men out of these kids after all!"

"Billy."

"Okay, gang, let's have a round of '*My Country Tis of Thee*'," Called Dad.

My Country Tis of Thee

Sweet land of liberty

Of thee I sing.

Land where my fathers died!

Land of the Pilgrims pride

From every mountainside

Let freedom ring!

"We haven't sounded that good since our first day on the road in Mexico. Okay kids, '*From the halls*'!"

From the halls of Montezuma

To the shores of Tripoli

We will fight our countries battles

In the air, on land and sea.

First to fight for right and freedom

And to keep our honor clean

We are proud to claim the title

Of United States Marines.

"What time is it anyway?" Melanie asked.

"Why ask what time it is? Aren't you having fun?" replied Dad.

"I'm having lots of fun. I'm worried about how long we'll be driving on the road at night in Mexico."

"Worry? Did I hear you say worry?" Dad acted astounded.

"No, thinking–about the road after dark."

"Leave the driving to us. Everything will work out fine." Dad smiled.

"What time is it, Billy?" Mother became curious too.

"It's only 5:30. There's plenty time yet before dark. Think about something else besides when we're going to get there."

Out came the Rosaries and Anne and Jimmy promptly flopped out.

Mom broke the silence afterward.

"It sure is good we had such a gigantic lunch. After getting up from the table this afternoon I thought I might never be able to eat another bite again in my life. I've never seen so much food. Have you ever?"

"They know how to do things, don't they? Doesn't look like anyone's dying of overwork either. I can't imagine coming home for lunch, having a meal like that and going back to work!" Dad said.

"It's hot and sunny all year round so they take a siesta in the hottest part of the day. It adds to the joie-de-vivre." I explained.

CHAPTER TWELVE

The best was yet to come.

The sun descended on the plains north of Saltillo. Dark roses, mauves, blues, amethyst, grey, pink and gold mixed and swirled in the evening sky.

"Only an hour's drive left, and we're back in the U.S.A. Hold on, sit tight."

The last traces of sunlight disappeared leaving a panoramic view of the Milky Way.

"Is anyone hungry yet?" Mother inquired.

"No way, Mom. Senora gave us enough courses for a week." I said.

"The Lord was looking out for us. She was an angel to have us. What a wonderful woman! I'm touched." Mom said.

Dad picked up speed, and then slowed down gradually. "Something's not right. The wagon's making noise." He said and continued slowing down till the car inched along. I observed smoke out of the window where the sunset had captured my attention.

"Will everyone please climb out of the car? Do what I tell you and climb out one by one. And do it now." Dad wore a grim countenance as he gave his orders.

"The car's still moving. Can you at least stop?" Jimmy protested. Dad kept the wagon creeping forward. Dad turned around and I knew there was definitely a problem.

"You heard me children. Do exactly what I said. Don't ask any questions – just climb out of the car one by one." He said.

I climbed out into the gravel by the side of the road and my sisters and brother followed making various noises as they plopped out of the moving vehicle.

By the time everyone was out the wagon was a block ahead of me and my sister Mel. Trudging forward to join the others I noticed my father pulling to a stop as flames began leaping up from the side of the wagon. Dad grabbed the water jug from the back seat and begin dousing the fire. It was under control in a few minutes but smoke continued to rise from the engine. Dad came and joined the rest of us huddled together under the starlight.

"This is really the middle of nowhere." I said. "There's nothing for miles around. In a few moments of quiet we stood together under the dark sky with only God to help us.

"It's curtains for us, now. What are we going to do Dad?" Jimmy whined.

"The engine was catching fire. That's why I told you all to get out. If I stopped suddenly it would have burst up even more, and you all would have panicked. I needed to stay calm but I guess you didn't have any idea why I was telling you to get out."

"Now Mother, can you honestly tell me 'it could be worse?'" Valerie asked.

"Yes, I certainly can. At least the car didn't burn up completely! Dad put the fire out and we're all here in one piece." She said. "It always could be worse."

"But now what are we going to do?" I asked. "I don't see any repair shops or hotels close by, do you?"

Anxiety hung in the air and no answer came.

"Let's put ourselves in God's hands. That's where we are anyway. Then we'll try to figure out what to do. He'll work this out." The rumbling of engines interrupted our praying. Headlights in the distance were coming up on us from the south in Saltillo. A group of cars seemed to be charging toward us at breakneck speed. Dad jumped in the driver's seat of the Ford wagon and switched on the hazard lights. Two cars whizzed by.

"I didn't think they'd stop. Anyway, I'm scared to death to meet whoever is on the road at this hour. Remember the warning about bandits? You can't...." I said. Before I finished Dad noticed the two cars stopping up ahead. They had been traveling at such high speed I thought there was an emergency. We kept an eye on them as they whizzed by, and to our surprise the two cars pulled to the side of the road then began to back up.

"Oh, ho. It's our good Samaritans. Keep thinking positive, gang!" boomed Dad.

"Who has been thinking positive?" asked Jim.

"It's not that bad, Jim. And it could be worse. One of you could've broken your arm or leg jumping out of the car." Dad replied, patting him on the back.

"Here goes nothing." Melanie said, nodding her head in to suggest that Dad take a look at what was going on in front of us on the shoulder.

The bride bundled with all her lace headgear and train stepped out of the taxi then the groom practically rolled out. The taxi driver marched back to speak to Dad but explanations were unnecessary. He said they would be glad to drive us up to the Police Station several miles ahead. The second vehicle inched backward and stopped. The parents of the bride and groom peered out of the window curiously. The driver of the first taxi went over to talk to them. They stopped laughing to listen to what he had to say then started up again after indicating their approval to the taxi driver. They were also most willing to drive the unfortunate travelers to safety.

The champagne at the wedding did its job. Everyone in their party was laughing uncontrollably. Melanie and I and Althea climbed into the vehicle with the bride and groom, joined by Liz and Jim. Everyone else climbed into the taxi with Dad and Mom. The cars took off in caravan. Moments later the taxi ahead accelerated and disappeared with our parents inside.

Mel and I had the fun car with the bride and groom. They seemed oblivious to us, as if they were using public transportation, and kept on laughing and cackling. It sounded almost as ridiculous as our foolishness along the highway. Their closeness had only just begun. My thoughts wandered into their future. I wondered what this closeness would turn into for them. I don't think I will forget this experience with a newly married couple. Why did I feel safe in a taxicab with strangers? Would I stop to pick up strangers on the night of my wedding? This is the second time the Guste family accepted charity today. These were Christian people. Drunk but Christian people. God's touching down again like when we prayed with the people at Mass in the Cathedral. It seemed normal for them to pick us up—all of us. I felt close to them in a way I can't ever forget. The best night in their life could've been the worst night in ours except for this beautiful shared humanity, and their natural acceptance of our company. It seemed like a crazy dream.

The Inspection Station and Border Police Headquarters was a thirty minute drive from the spot where the old Ford blew up. Stepping out of the taxicab, I wished the new couple all sorts of closeness as they headed off into marvelous unknowns ahead.

The Mexican Government Inspection Station, stark and dreary, conjured images of a Communist country. A bare stucco wall like the one at the restaurant in Saltillo. The place felt like a prison room where you met with your lawyer. The taxi driver explained our situation to the officers on duty and they immediately began making phone calls. They needed a tow truck from Laredo, and they were willing to wake the dead mechanics in the area or be forced to face entertaining us in the vacant waiting room for the night.

"What time is it? Aren't we all getting a little tired?" Mother asked, for once in her life blurting something counterproductive.

"No use thinking about it. We're stuck here until we can get the car towed across the border. We're only a half-hour away from Laredo." Dad said.

"The Ford is a half hour back that way and all our things are on top!" Mom was aghast.

"There's nothing we can do about that, either." He said.

"You can't take it with you!" I commented, trying to help.

"I might lose my best shorts and toothbrush!" Mel said and looked around at everyone.

"Cheer up, everybody, it could be worse!" said Liz.

"It could not." Said Anne. "When are we going to get past Mexico?"

"Soon, honey. Very soon. In fact, Anne, tonight we will GET PAST MEXICO! Now come on over here. Let's sit and wait in peace. We have a lot to thank God for." Mom said.

"We already said the Rosary, so we don't need to do that again, Mother." I said.

"I'll take the rest of them outside. You can hold onto Anne in here." Mother took Anne beside her on the chairs lined up against the grey stucco walls and cuddled her to sleep.

Dad climbed into the tow truck cabin a while later and I offered to go along. He said no, to help Mom here. Thankfully, Anne had been able to sleep. I wondered what would it be like if everything were stolen off the top of the wagon, when we would get in a bed, and was Dad safe going alone with that husky guy who had his sleep disturbed to come rescue us at the border station? What if the guy hates Americans?

I led the younger ones outdoors, and the dark of night quietly enfolded us in mystery. Huddling under bright stars, I embraced all the closeness Mom loved so much.

And some of the maxims made more sense out here. What's the use of worrying? I began to understand it – there is none. It took coming to this point, but I understand it now.

"Who remembers anything from astronomy? Did anyone get to that in school?" I asked.

"Why don't we sing 'Whenever I feel Afraid?'" Mel said.

"You feel afraid?" I said.

"Of course not. I thought it'd be a good song though." Mel smiled at me.

Whenever I feel afraid, I hold my head erect

And whistle a happy tune, so no one will suspect

I'm afraid.

"I want *'Tell me Why'* from campfire time." Came Val.

Tell me why the stars do shine

Tell me why the ivy twines

Tell me why the skies are blue

And I will tell you why I love you.

"Too mushy! It's disgusting." Jimmy said. "I see a snake over there! I'm not kidding either. Watch out."

"What a brat, making that up." Allie said, looking where he pointed.

"I just heard the rattle. Oh my God here it comes." Liz screeched.

"Look for a stick to clobber it with." I said. "Everyone yell for the policeman in there."

Melanie and I grabbed sticks lying in the grass and beat the ground in front of the rattlesnake to forbid it to come further. The policeman arrived, signaled to us to go back inside, and took care of the rattlesnake with his pistol.

Back inside, Liz put in a request for "*Taps.*"

Day is done. Gone the sun.

From the lakes, from the hills, from the sky.

All is well, safely rest, God is nigh.

"What was all that commotion out there?" Mother asked, looking up.

"A four foot long rattlesnake. Nothing to worry about." I said.

"The Taps was lovely. You girls sing nicely." She said, tipping her head back.

"A rattlesnake wide enough to enjoy one of us for dinner." I said.

"Thank God all of you are okay." She said, pulling out smelling salts. "What time is it?" She looked up at the clock. "Two?" She pulled out her Rosary.

Mother's face became increasingly grim, even through her Rosary.

"Don't let it get you, Mom. I know what you're worried about. Just take it with a grain of salt. Water off a duck's back. Just like you're always telling us." I said.

"I want your father back here soon. This has been too long. He should be back by now."

"There's nothing you can do about it right now. We'll make it."

Two thirty a.m. the tow truck pulling the wagon appeared.

"Most of you can travel inside the wagon. A few of us can join the driver in the truck cab. Who wants to join me in front?" Dad said.

There was no contest. I volunteered.

During the drive up to Laredo, it was quiet, and though curious how it had gone back there with his getting the wagon, I didn't ask a thing. He would never have admit it if the guy had given him trouble.

As the hours of night disappeared things seemed surreal and the campers were punchy. The pendulum would swing – first the nightmare feeling, then the circus, then the horror show, then the laugh riot. Blurry moments of exhaustion were punctuated with moments of fear. Leaning on Dad's shoulder in the truck cab, my brain replayed the previous three hours. Could I ever describe all that happened? And the things I learned in such a short time? I woke up with Dad's arm around my shoulder.

Then to customs station. I get was getting sloppy, feeling nutty, and disoriented. Are they really going to undo all our stuff again? Even if they have to climb on top of the tow truck and on top of the wagon to pull it all out and down. Yep, that seems exactly what those brutes are going for. The drill was to bring out each and every tote. This is going to take years! It's past our bedtime! During the wait, I leaned on my father's shoulder in the truck cab, going in and out of sleep. I wondered is this a dream. Is it a tunnel we fell into, like Alice falling into the tunnel under the tree? I tried to grab hold of myself, tell myself I wasn't falling apart, tell myself I was perfectly alright. Everything will go back to normal. We will be in our hotel soon. We will go to bed. We will be in the U.S.A. We will be able to eat our usual food. Don't let these guys get you. Don't let it get you.

I climbed out of the truck cab and went to check on the travelers inside the inclined wagon. Anne had fallen asleep on Mother's lap. Jimmy was crashed on her left shoulder. Mother's head was tilted toward the window. She looked seasick.

Liz began reciting. "My bonnie lies over the ocean. My bonnie lies over the sea. My bonnie lies over the ocean. O bring back my bonnie to me."

"Are you going crazy too?" I asked.

"You might say that." She answered.

"You all look seasick." I said.

"Yes, I am seasick."

"I am dying, Mal." Valerie announced with a sentimental goodbye in her voice.

"Really?" I asked, smiling.

"Really." She said.

"Of what?" I asked.

"Claustro...er...excuse me. A disease that doesn't exist." There were five people huddled in the middle seat practicing togetherness.

"You got to ride up there in the truck." Allie remarked. "It was awful riding in this station wagon. Bumpy, and we were tilted over."

"I got to ride in the truck? No one wanted to ride with Dad. The driver didn't say one word or crack a smile the entire ride. It wasn't good either, let me tell you." I said.

"When we shove off from Customs, you can have the chance to ride in here and get seasick, Mal. Come on, get in."

The customs officers surrounded the inclined wagon with powerful flashlights and I shut tight my eyes until I knew they were finished. The feeling of degradation and humiliation stretched the moments.

"Oh, God, you've got to be kidding." Liz coughed.

"Couldn't they tell what we've been through tonight?" I complained. These were not the Christians of Mexico. Their boss wasn't too Christian either. You would think Castro took over here! They act like we're the enemy.

"I wish I could say we look like nice people, but we don't." Mom said.

"No sense wondering what we look like to them." I added.

"Who cares?" Mel said.

"There are a lot of people smuggling things into the country. Maybe that's why these guys have to be so strict." I said.

"Get me out of here." Val said climbing out of the wagon. She stared at the men at work in our personal belongings and got back in, sticking her head out of the window to gulp the musty night air.

"How about *Kumbaya*?"

Laredo 6 AM. Our driver pulled to a stop in front of The Laredo Hotel. Right in the town center, the façade appeared to be as old as anything you could find in the area. A protruding marquis displayed the familiar AAA symbol. "Welcome. No Refrigeration." The unfriendly escort who had driven us from the Inspection Station got out of the truck cab and mopped his forehead. Dad climbed out behind him, and came over to the inclined Ford to discuss the situation with Mother.

"It's past 6 o'clock, Butz. This isn't what you're used to but I think this driver needs to go home. He's still needs to get the wagon over to his repair shop and unload. This'll have to be it." Mother winced and shrugged her shoulders, turned around towards us, silently expressing resignation.

"We'll do better tomorrow night. At least we've made it across the border." He went in to check in to the Laredo.

Mother carried Anne through the hotel doors. Dad took Jimmy and followed. In the elevator, everyone was quiet, attentive, resigned, ready to crash. Dad turned the key and we piled through the door to our room. Everyone found a place, yanked back covers and crawled in without thinking about pajamas. The room went quiet then Anne broke the hush.

"I need another pair of underwear, Mom." She stated, looking up sheepishly. Fits of laughter broke out immediately.

"We're dying of fatigue finally getting to our rooms, and Anne says she needs another pair of underwear! Have you lost your marbles, Anne? What makes you think Mom can find you another pair of underwear at a time like this anyway?" Elizabeth teased and everyone was back to wide awake.

That was a night, or truthfully a morning, that dying of laughter became an honest-to-God possibility. It might've been the best medicine at any other time, but on that night it seemed potentially fatal.

"I'm not sleeping with Anne. She needs new underwear for a reason." Said Elizabeth. "You get the cot." She glared over at Anne and burst out laughing.

"Hey, I never thought of that one." Said Val. "What's your problem, Anne?"

"I'm keeping it to myself this time." Anne folded back the sheets.

Dad and Mother came in for prayers and we thanked God we had found our way to safety, if not comfort.

"Can you believe it was just today that we had lunch at the Camillieri's ranch? It seems like that was two days ago." Mel remarked soberly, "So much happened in the meantime." Somewhat dazed, still kneeling, she lay her head on the twin bed.

"Everybody under the covers!" Dad said.

"Under the covers? There's no refrigeration in here!" Val pouted.

"We made it back to the States. Don't complain."

"Our international experience is coming to an end." Mel added dryly.

Once Mom and Dad left the room and the door was shut behind them, I fastened the bolt and chain. "We've been through enough for one night. I'm not taking any chances on another surprise." I said.

"Yeah, that driver seemed so disgusted and aggravated with us, he might send a friend to give us trouble like we gave him." Melanie conjured up early morning nightmares.

"Don't talk about negative ideas!" said Liz. "I need some sleep."

"Maybe the rattlesnake stowed away in the station wagon." Allie chuckled.

"Anne, guess what! We're finally PAST MEXICO!" Valerie cheered.

"I didn't want to hurt Dad's feelings but I'm glad we made it back, period. It's a relief to be back in the United States!" I said.

"You bet it is!" Said Valerie.

"I agree." Mel added.

"Me too." Came Althea.

"Me three." Chirped Anne.

"What an adventure this has been! It hardly seems like it was all real. So many things happened that we could never forget. It's like a dream is coming to an end." I marveled wistfully.

"Could you ever forget that welcoming committee of burly fellows going topless at that first Pemex station?" Valerie added.

"I'll never forget the ride down that inclined street in Quanajuato with the peddlers sticking their noses in the car and the Toyota coming towards us." Melanie smiled with amusement.

"And the look on that waiter's face when we ordered Chateaubriand and champagne in the castle after closing time." Liz hooted.

"How about getting the President's suite at the Alameda!" Jimmy crowed triumphantly.

"And Mom buying those three huge lamps to crowd up the back of the car!" Val shook her head. Chuckles broke into laughs.

"And the look on that waiters face when Dad turned from his raffle game to ask for the wine menu!" I added.

"What about the time Mal had to go in the grass on the highway?" Jim hooted.

"And remember poor Alfredo flirting with Mother? Maybe he felt sorry for her."

"And the frog stories!" Anne chimed.

"That hotel in Saltillo with the septic tank out back?" Melanie laughed.

"Was that what it was?" I wondered out loud.

"Remember the Bell Captain at the Alameda suggesting we couldn't afford to stay there?" Liz broke out.

"And Mom's face when she found out we had box seats for the bullfight?" My glasses fell off the bedside table. That was the point when death by laughter became a possibility. We have to stop this. "Stop laughing everybody. I can't breathe! I am dying of laughter." All this closeness. It was fun, but I might die of it too.

"What's funny about my glasses falling off the bedside table?" The roaring escalated a notch.

"Calm down and let's get some sleep. I'm going to die if we don't stop this. It's near sunrise. Quiet down." The escalation only continued.

"We're so punchy. This has been the longest night of my life." Said Liz.

"The longest trip of my life." Said Anne.

"I never want to see another tortilla chip in my life." Said Jimmy. "Or another Pemex bathroom."

"Go to sleep." I said.

"I'm hot." Said Jim.

"There's no refrigeration in The Laredo Hotel. Forget it." Mel said.

"Water off a duck's back." Said Allie.

"No—water off a boy's back." Replied Jim.

There came a knock at the door. A hush fell over the group. Fear descended into the room. Melanie and I sat straight up and pricked our ears. Another two quiet raps and I got up to put my ear to the door.

"Whose there?" I said, my stomach in a knot.

"It's Mother." Came the reply.

"Oh." I unlocked the door and pulled it open, forgetting the chain latch, which prevented it opening the rest of the way. Before I could close and open it fully, Mom stuck her hand through the crack. Dangling from her drooping hand was a pair of ladies' nylon underwear.

"For Anne." She said.

At the breakfast table in the diner of The Laredo, Anne sipped Coke and nibbled on crackers. I satisfied myself with Saltine's too, and they never tasted so delicious. The distress of the previous evening had wreaked its havoc on my intestines.

"I can't believe Memere has been suffering with stomach trouble for years. I'd have died by now." I remarked, looking over over at Mel's open menu. "I'm starved, but I'm not about to take a chance. We have a long day's drive ahead." The waitress arrived and pulled out her pad.

"Don't worry, Ma'am. At least three of the girls won't be having breakfast. I'll have two plain scrambled eggs, toast and coffee. Valerie, you go next."

"I'll take a scrambled egg, toast and orange juice." Valerie said and popped shut the menu.

"It's great to be in America ordering breakfast in English!" said Liz.

"What would you like, Liz?" Mom prompted.

"Rice Krispies and a glass of milk." She smiled and closed the menu.

"I'll take pancakes and orange juice." Jim smiled.

"Wonderful. Melanie?" Mom asked.

"A scrambled egg and some orange juice, please." She replied.

Anne and I were still feeling the shadow of Montezuma's ghost. Mother passed her glance to me, and I held up a pack of crackers. Anne nodded to Mom and pointed to the pack of crackers.

"I'd like another coke, please." Anne said.

"I'll take one, too." I added.

Althea was poring over the menu with great interest. You might have thought she was studying illustrations of rare birds in the encyclopedia

"What about you, Althea?" Mother interrupted her studies gently.

Althea looked up and uttered her fantastic conclusion. "I think I'll have the tacos!"

"Oh no you won't." Mother slapped the menu shut. "We won't be having tacos for a while. She threw a glance at the waitress. "One more egg and toast, please."

Mother drove home across Texas going fifty miles per hour, as per instructions from the mechanic in Laredo. There were song fests, history lessons, the Rosary, skirmishes, bathroom stops, lost shoe emergencies, map searches, pranks, naptime. I picked up *How to Stop Worrying and Start Living*. Did someone I know write this book? Someone in this car?

"Come on, gang." He boomed out. "We've made it to Airline Highway! Let's have a verse of 'Pack up your Troubles'!

Pack up your troubles in your old kit bag

And smile, smile, smile!

If you've a lucifer to light your fag,

Smile boys that's the style!

What's the use of worrying?

It never was worthwhile. So...

Pack up you troubles in your old kit bag, and

Smile, smile, smile.

The End

About the Author

A native of New Orleans, Louisiana, Marie Louise Nix was graduated from the Academy of the Sacred Heart and from Manhattanville College (N.Y.) She pursued theological studies in the Andover Newton Consortium in Boston, then attained her J.D. degree from Loyola University School of Law.

Ms. Nix is the author of three books of poetry and photography including *Visions of Splendor: Poems and Images of the Beyond in our Midst*, *Transportation to the Higher Place*, *Restoring Soul: Poems of Healing, Encounter, Awareness and Empowerment*. She also authored *Being There: Reflections from the Scenes of the Mysteries of the Rosary*.

Marie Louise has been active in the formation and development of several initiatives promoting literacy and access to resources for all members of her community. She currently serves as an Advisory Board member for the St. Tammany Parish Library Foundation. She is an active member of the Northlake Literary Society and a member of the Legacy Campaign for the Harry Tompson Center for the Homeless in New Orleans.

Ms. Nix is the mother of five grown children. Her lifetime hobbies include spending time with family, choral singing, swimming, travel and cooking. She lives in Madisonville, Louisiana.

A portion of the proceeds of each book will be shared with The Harry Tompson Center for the Homeless in New Orleans, LA or the 2nd Harvest Food Bank.

Children of William Joseph Guste, Jr. and Dorothy Schutten Guste

William Joseph Guste, III, Attorney-at-Law, New Orleans LA Married to Maureen Kerrigan Guste. 6 children, 17 grandchildren.

Bernard Randolph Guste, Restaurateur. Served as Proprietor of Antoine's Restaurant in New Orleans for 20 years. His beautiful bride Henrietta Vinas Guste resides in heaven. 4 children, 9 grandchildren.

Marie Louise Guste Nix, Attorney and Author of *All This Closeness*. Biographical info enclosed. 5 children, 2 grandchildren.

Melanie Anne Guste, R.S.C.J. (Religious of the Sacred Heart). 7 years Headmistress of the Academy of the Sacred Heart in New Orleans.

Valerie Guste Johnson. Married to Robert Paul Johnson. Foundress and Director of Keys for the Homeless a 501c3 providing needed supplies to the homeless in the Washington D.C. area. 6 Children, 4 grandchildren.

Althea Guste Wise, Realtor. Married to Jonathan Wise, M.D. 4 Children, 4 grandchildren.

Elizabeth Therese Guste, Accountant for major Film Productions. A health and wellness expert and business owner.

James Patrick Guste, In Management at Antoine's Restaurant. 2 children.

Anne Duchesne Guste, Attorney and Author of "Stories of My Mother and The General's Cookbook."

www.ingramcontent.com/pod-product-compliance
Lightning Source LLC
Chambersburg PA
CBHW020525270326
41927CB00006B/447

* 9 7 8 0 9 7 0 2 5 6 3 4 8 *